AF226053

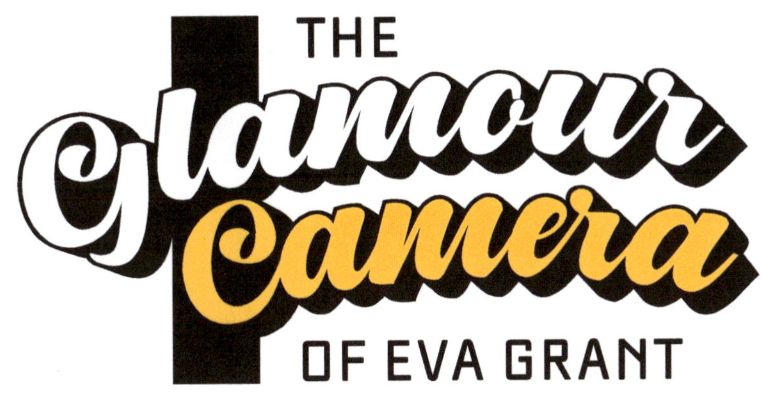

THE
Glamour
Camera
OF EVA GRANT

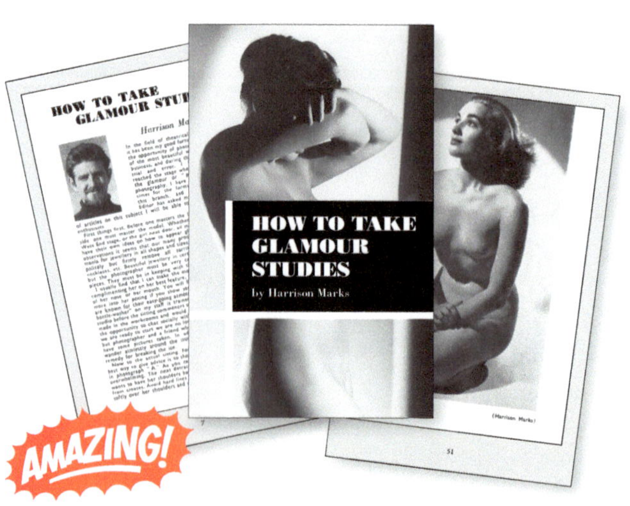

AMAZING!

Receive a **FREE** copy of
How to take Glamour Studies by Harrison Marks
when you sign up to our mailing list at
www.pamela-green.com/mailing-list

Published in 2023 by Wolfbait Books
www.wolfbait.co.uk

ISBN: 978-1-9162151-8-4

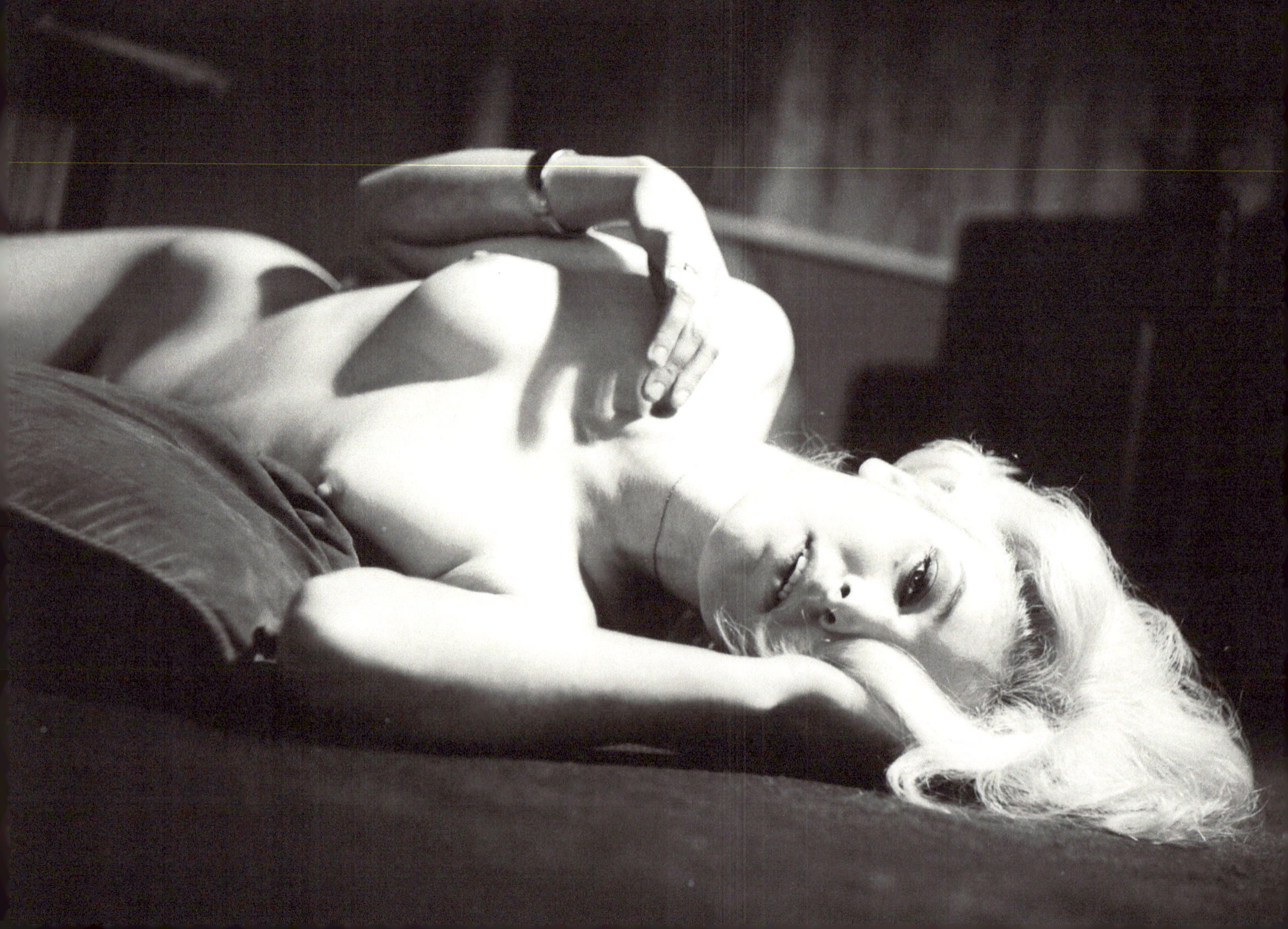

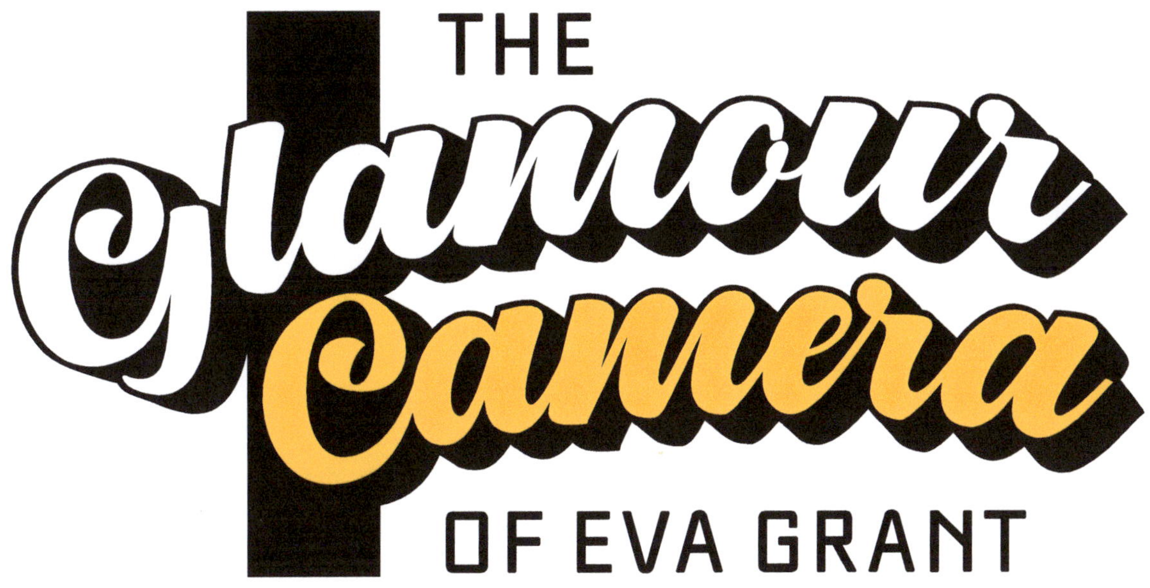

By Yahya El-Droubie

Photography by Eva Grant

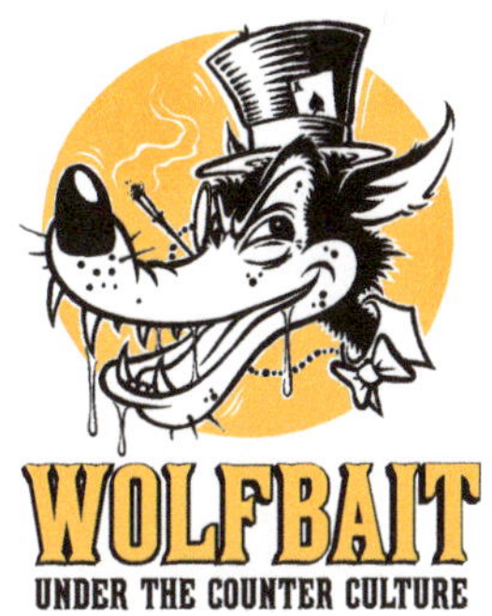

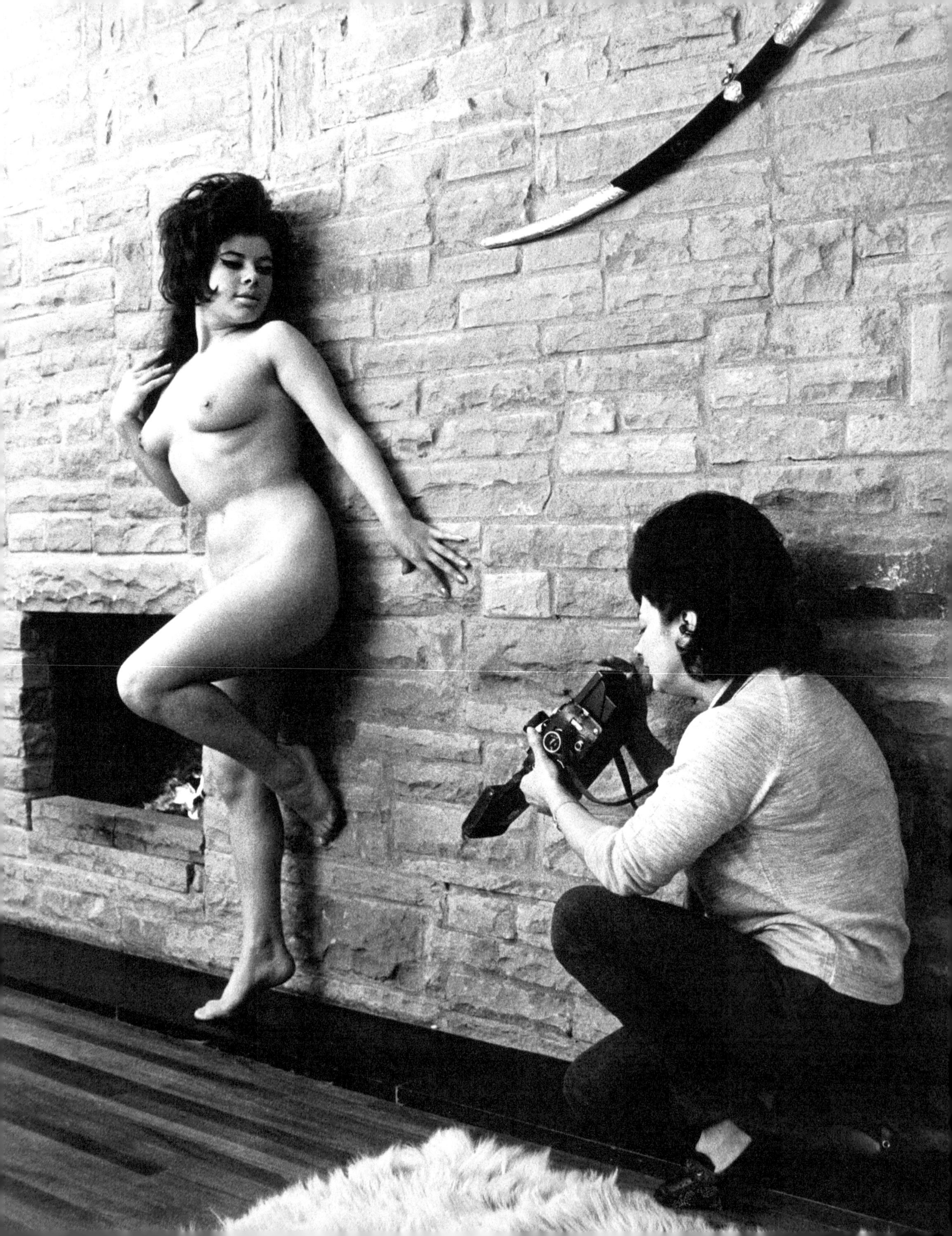

All About Eva

EVA GRANT WAS ONE OF the most gifted glamour photographers of the 1950s and early 1960s. She was born in 1925 in Istanbul, Turkey, to Greek parents; in the 1930s, the family returned to Greece and settled in the capital, Athens, where Eva spent the Second World War and her formative and teenage years. An avid Anglophile, Eva wanted to travel to England when the war ended; she would have done anything to achieve her ambition, but as an unmarried young woman, it took her a long time to persuade her father to let her leave.

One day, she spotted a recruitment advertisement for student nurses in London and applied for a place at the nursing school. However, the response was so slow that in the interim she also applied for a job as an air hostess at TAE, the Greek national airline. "Back then, it was the biggest thing for a Greek girl to be an air hostess," Eva recalled. "But for me, it was a way to come to England. They were advertising for presentable young ladies. They saw us in bikinis under the guise of saving people in the water."

Eva then received a letter of acceptance from the nursing school, and, at the age of 22, she dropped everything and moved to London. Once she'd settled in, she supplemented her income as a student nurse at Shenley Hospital – a psychiatric institution in Hertfordshire – by doing the occasional assignment as a swimwear model. Shenley, which was redeveloped for housing in the 1990s, was sited just five miles from Spielplatz nudist colony in Bricket Wood.

In time, an amateur photographer spotted Eva's swimwear photos and asked her to pose for him; this work, for which she was paid more in one hour than she earned in a week as a nurse, led to a little figure work. But Eva found modelling boring and became intrigued by what was going on behind the camera. "Photographers were happy to share their knowledge with me as it was so rare for the model to be interested," she recalled.

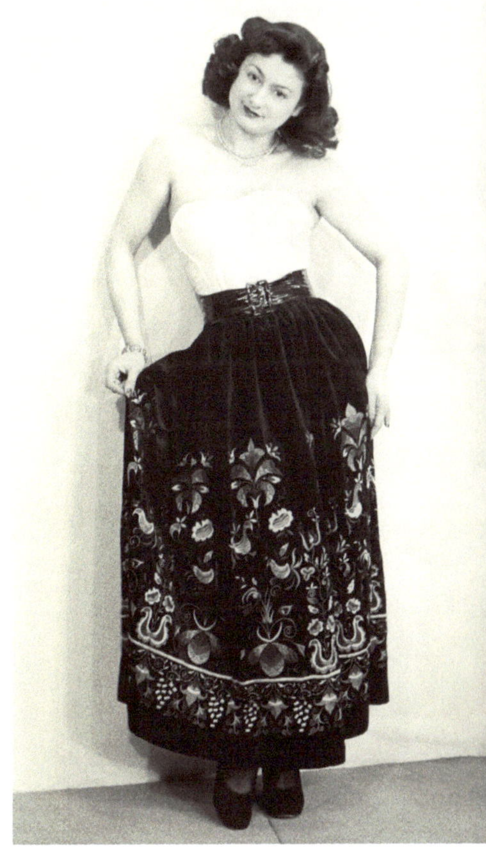

Above: Eva Grant.

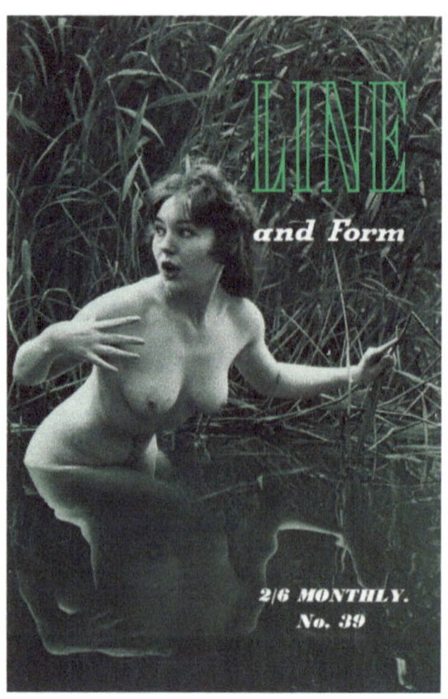

Above: Sally Ann Scott on the cover of *Line and Form* no. 39.

Opposite: A contact sheet; the model is Diane Du Bois.

The urge to portray the female figure is as old as man himself, and when he scratched on the walls of his cave to immortalise his hairy mate, little did he know that he would lay the foundation for a most fascinating form of Art.

— Eva Grant

Around this time, Eva married her first husband, an electrical engineer who had just graduated from Durham University. As a side hustle to earn some extra cash, the couple photographed people at functions. "My husband would take the pictures and rush off to have them developed while I was looking beautiful and talking to the people, and then he would come back and sell them," Eva said.

The newlyweds were offered a basement flat with a darkroom attached, which they accepted eagerly and hired out as a studio to amateur photographers to help pay the rent. "One day, I saw a model and thought: What a gorgeous face she's got," Eva said. "When I saw the photographer's results, though, I thought, I can do better than that. So, I photographed her."

At the suggestion of a friend, Eva submitted the photograph to a magazine, and much to her surprise, they accepted it and asked for more. Glamour, bikini shots and figure studies soon followed, and a company, Eva Grant Ltd, was instituted. At this stage of her career, most of Eva's commissions were from British and French magazines, including *Paris Hollywood*. Every eight weeks, she would travel to the French capital to submit new work and pick up a cheque.

In the glamour industry of the 1950s and 1960s women photographers were rare; Yvonne Gregory and Joan Craven were of an earlier British generation, and in the United States there was Bunny Yeager. Despite this, Eva felt that being a woman was an advantage in the field: "I was successful with my pictures of girls because as I was a woman, they didn't feel threatened, and I could talk to them about boyfriends and such and get them to relax."

Like fellow glamour photographers George Harrison Marks and Russell Gay, as her business grew, Eva published her own pocket magazine; called *Line and Form* it ran for more than 40 issues and was produced under her own imprint, Photoform. A lot of the women Eva photographed in her work were not professional models – they were amateurs hoping to turn pro or typists wanting to make a bit of extra cash; several were dancers who Eva loved working with as they had natural grace and could hold a pose. The professional models Rosa Dolmai, June Palmer and Lee Sothern (aka Grace Jackson) all posed for her, too.

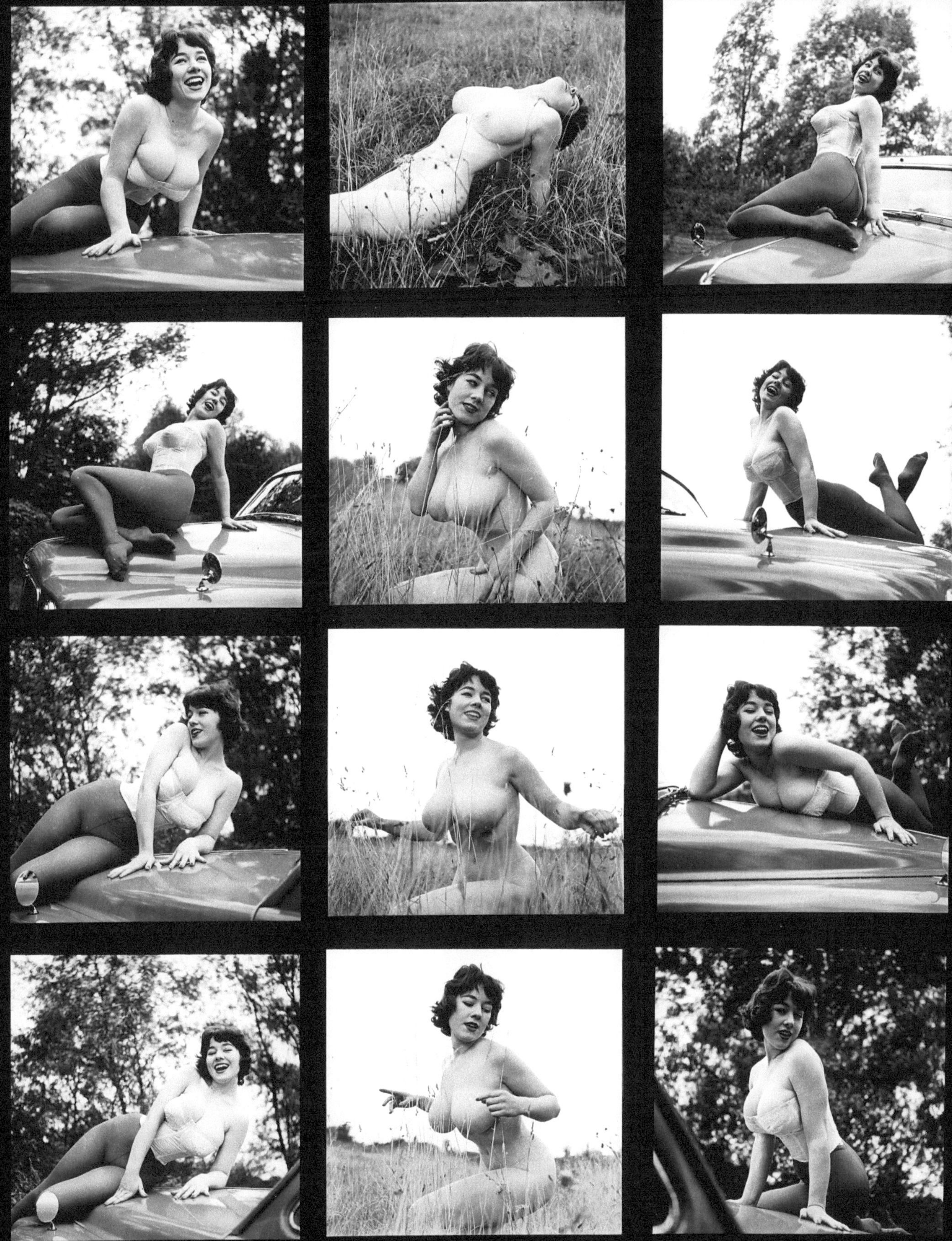

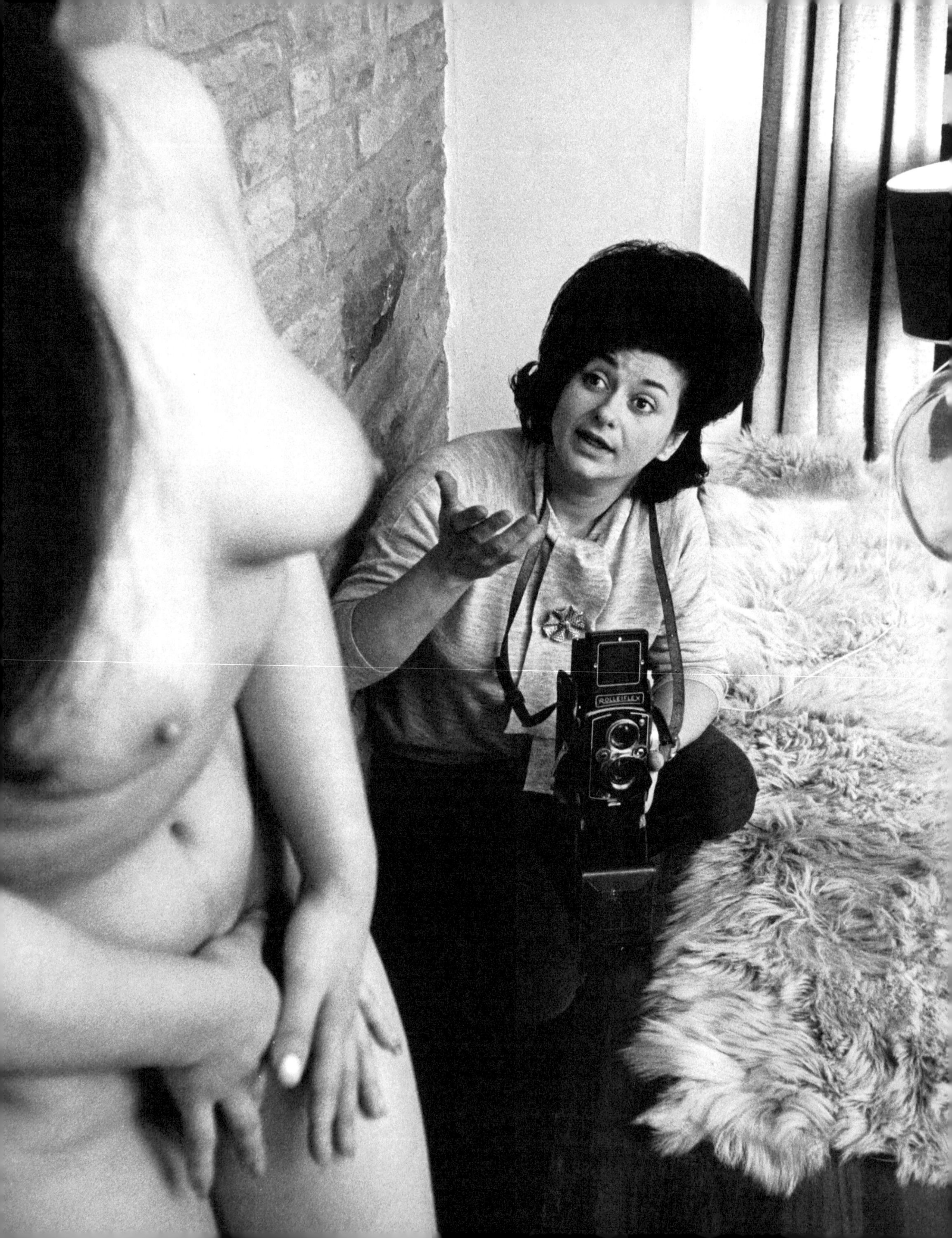

Many of the photoshoots took place in the models' own bedsits. Eva wouldn't know what these were like until she arrived there, and she often had to make do with suboptimal conditions. She would usually look for straight lines in a background to contrast with the softness and curves of the girls' figures. Almost all the models were shot using natural light, sometimes using a sheet as a reflector.

Other shoots took place outdoors, where being spotted by members of the public was a constant hazard. "I used to take a model to a location in Kew [in southwest London] at 5 or 6 am, before there would be people around. She would wear a big coat and nothing else. I had to work very fast. If I saw anyone coming, she'd put her coat back on. The trouble was, the light wasn't very good because it was so early. One day I was working with five girls at Walton-on-the-Naze [in Essex]. It was very early and freezing cold, and they were shivering. I said, 'Well, at least your nipples will stand up!'"

Eva also worked at a nudist colony at Sunbury-on-Thames in Surrey, where she was the only person present wearing clothes. To protect herself from the UK's obscenity laws, Eva hired a lawyer, who would sanction her prints by stamping them on the back as appropriate.

In 1956, Eva visited New York to see the work of US glamour photographers. The *London Evening Standard* ran the story: "Photographer Eva Grant goes to New York armed with hundreds of pictures of beautiful girls to take America by storm." She found most US photography over-posed and stylised; however, the best of it, such as the work of Andre de Dienes, Peter Gowland and Peter Basch, was to her very exciting and impressive: "Flawless taste, faultless technique, a refined sense of animal symmetry and natural lighting," she declared.

— Eva Grant

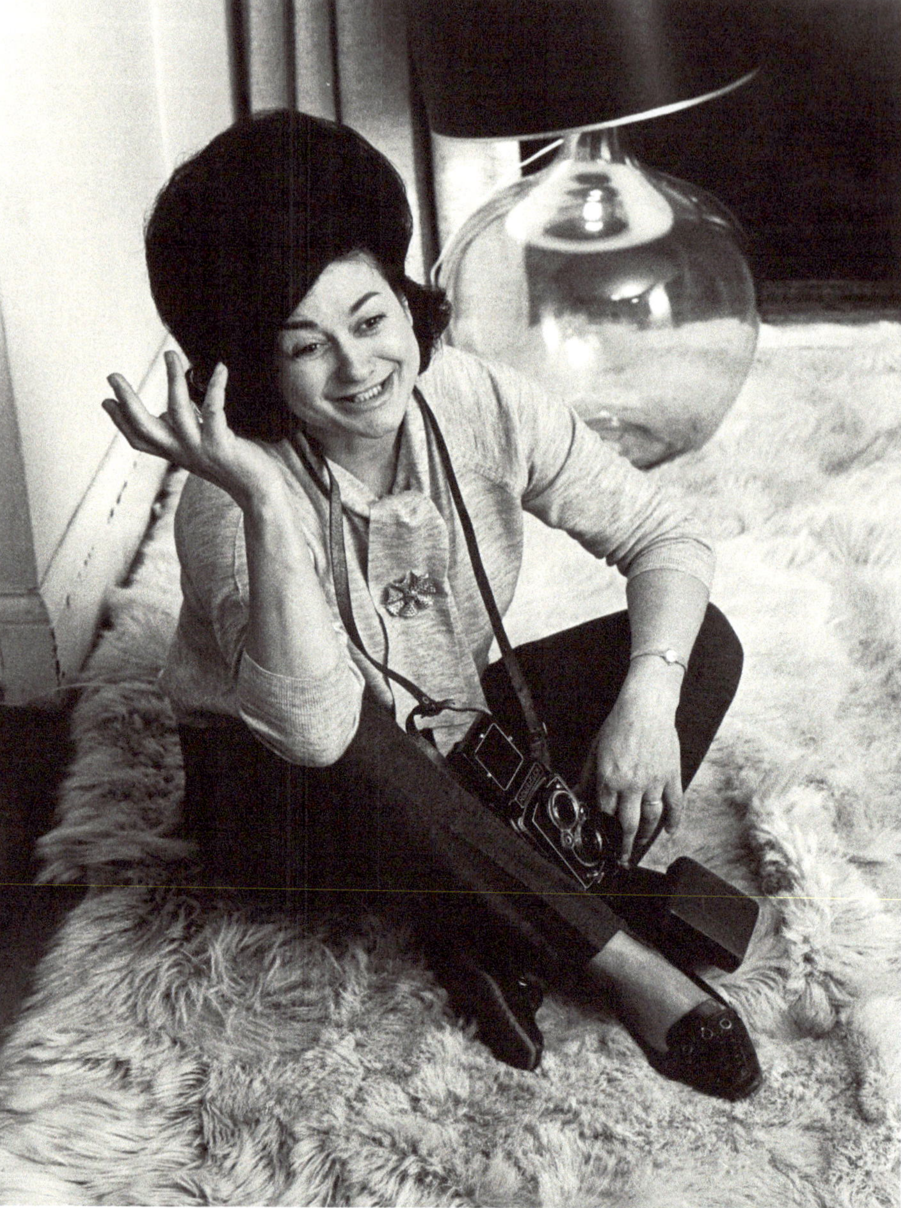

Right: Eva Grant taking a break.

When Eva returned to England, it was no more models in bedsits for her. But what worked for the US market wouldn't necessarily work for the French or German markets. The Germans liked healthy outdoor images; the Americans liked their cheesecake; and the French liked things a little saucy. The audience for these pictures was primarily male, and it was within all these parameters that Eva had to find her voice and personal style. Her work appeared regularly in American photography magazines, such as those published by Fawcett and Whitestone – *Glamour Photos*, *Camera Studies of Figure Beauty* and *Salon Photography*.

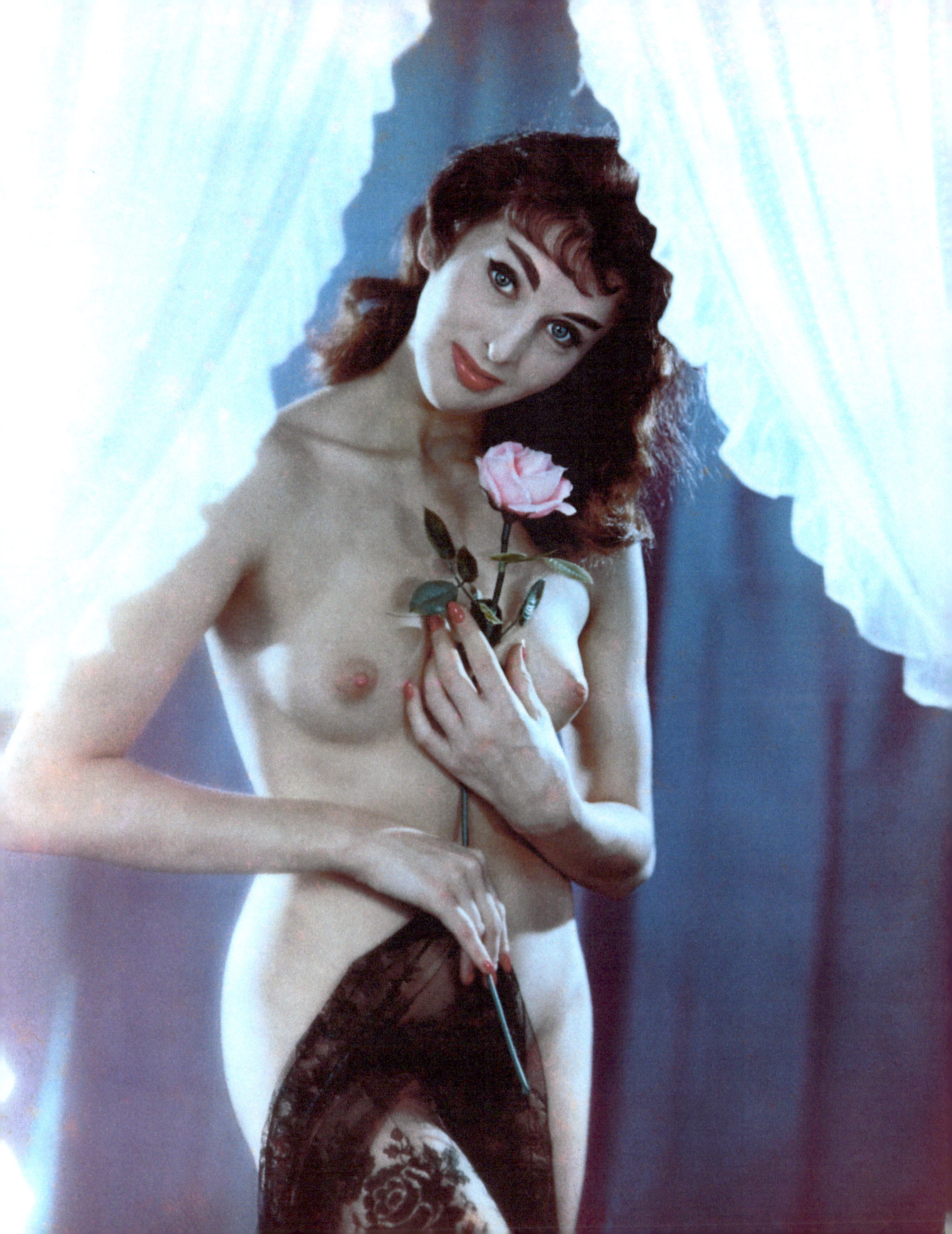

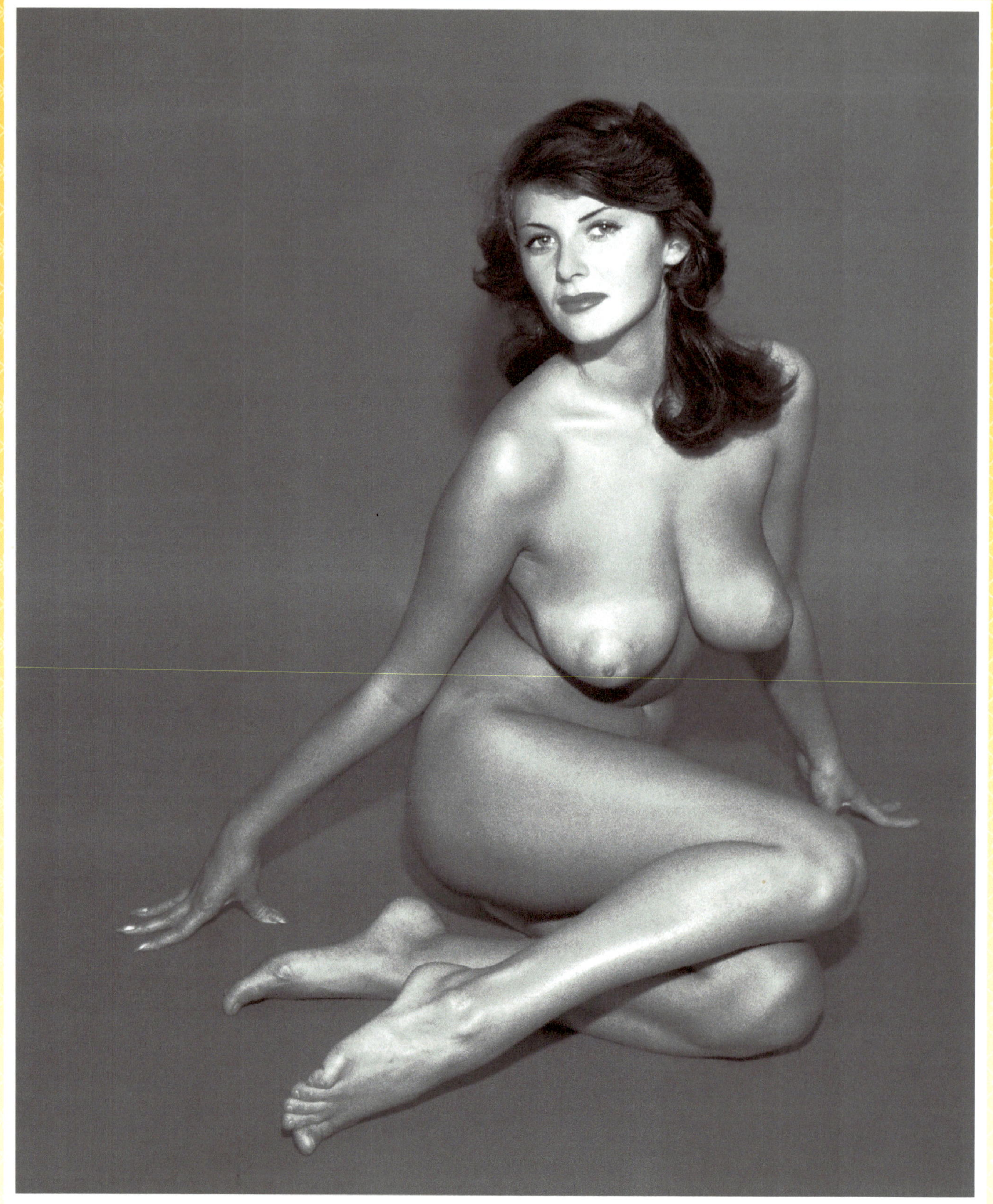

However, by the mid-1960s, the heyday of figure studies and innocent glamour work was coming to an end. "Magazines wanted hotter and hotter pictures, with poses that were more explicit than I was prepared to do," Eva said. "Soft porn was a big jump then, not like now. So, I decided to call it a day."

In 1964, Eva gave up photography and sold her studio; shortly afterwards, she had her fourth child. During the 1970s, she became a tour guide for the London Tourist Board, a job she continued to do into the 1980s. She separated from her first husband and married Lord Hatch of Lusby (1917–1992), a prominent anti-apartheid campaigner. Travelling to Africa with him, Eva met political leaders such as Kenneth Kaunda and Nelson Mandela; the couple considered the latter to be a friend.

Now in her late nineties, Eva Grant lives in Kew in southwest London.

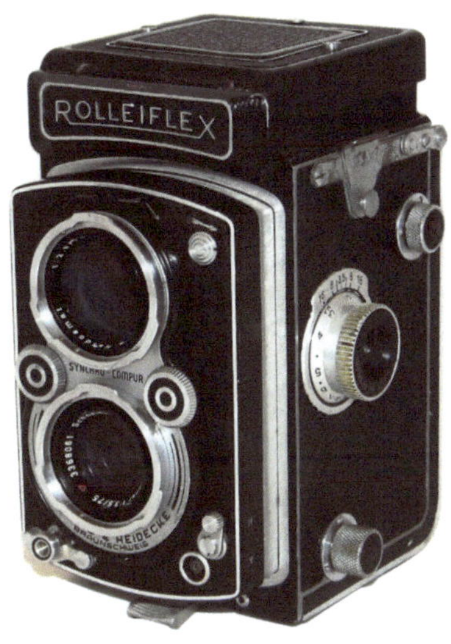

Above: Eva Grant's camera of choice: the Rolleiflex Automat Type 4 TLR, Xenar 75 3.5 lens, made in Germany 1951–1954.

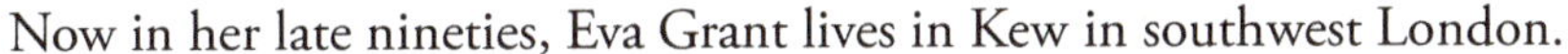

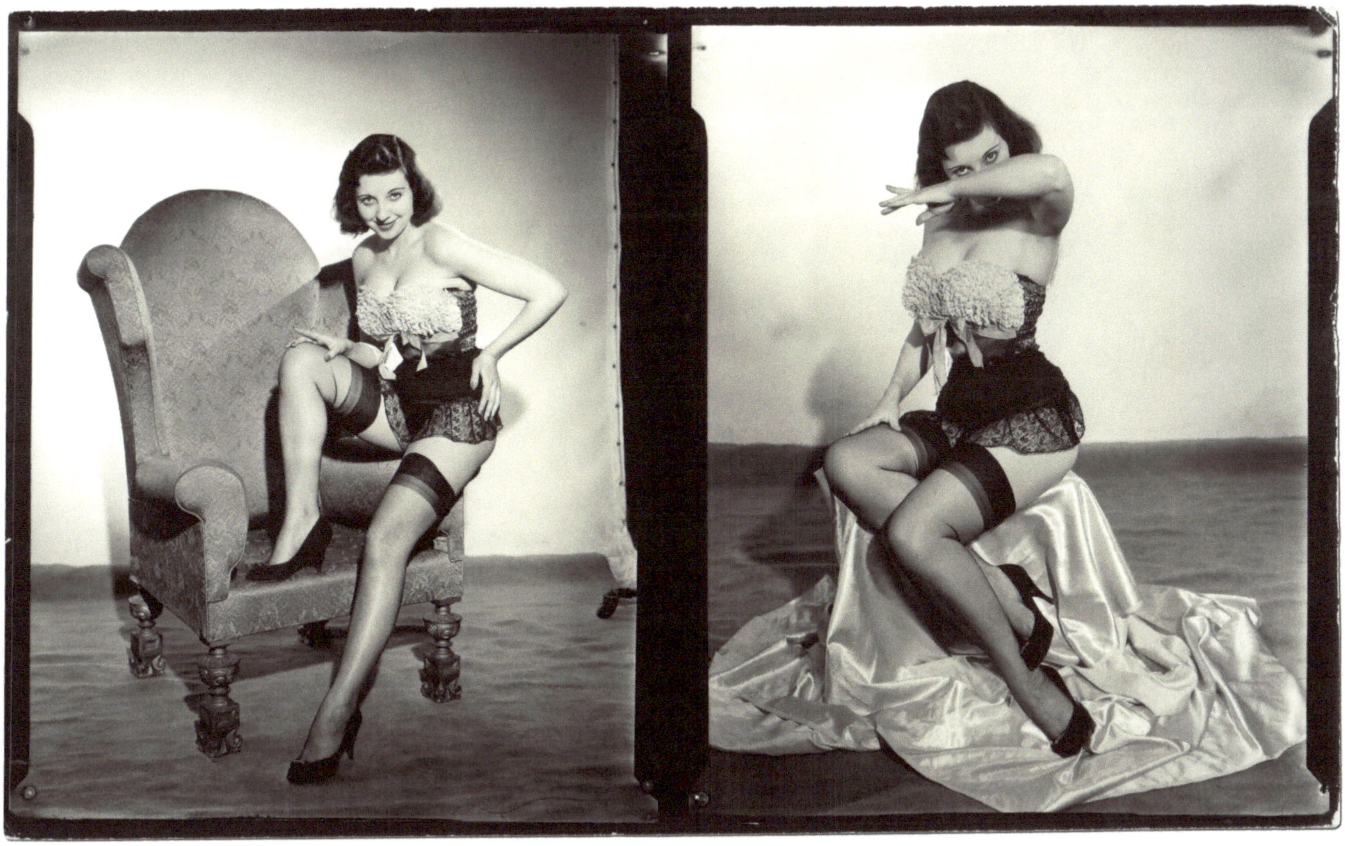

Above: A large-format contact sheet, circa 1950s. Model unknown.

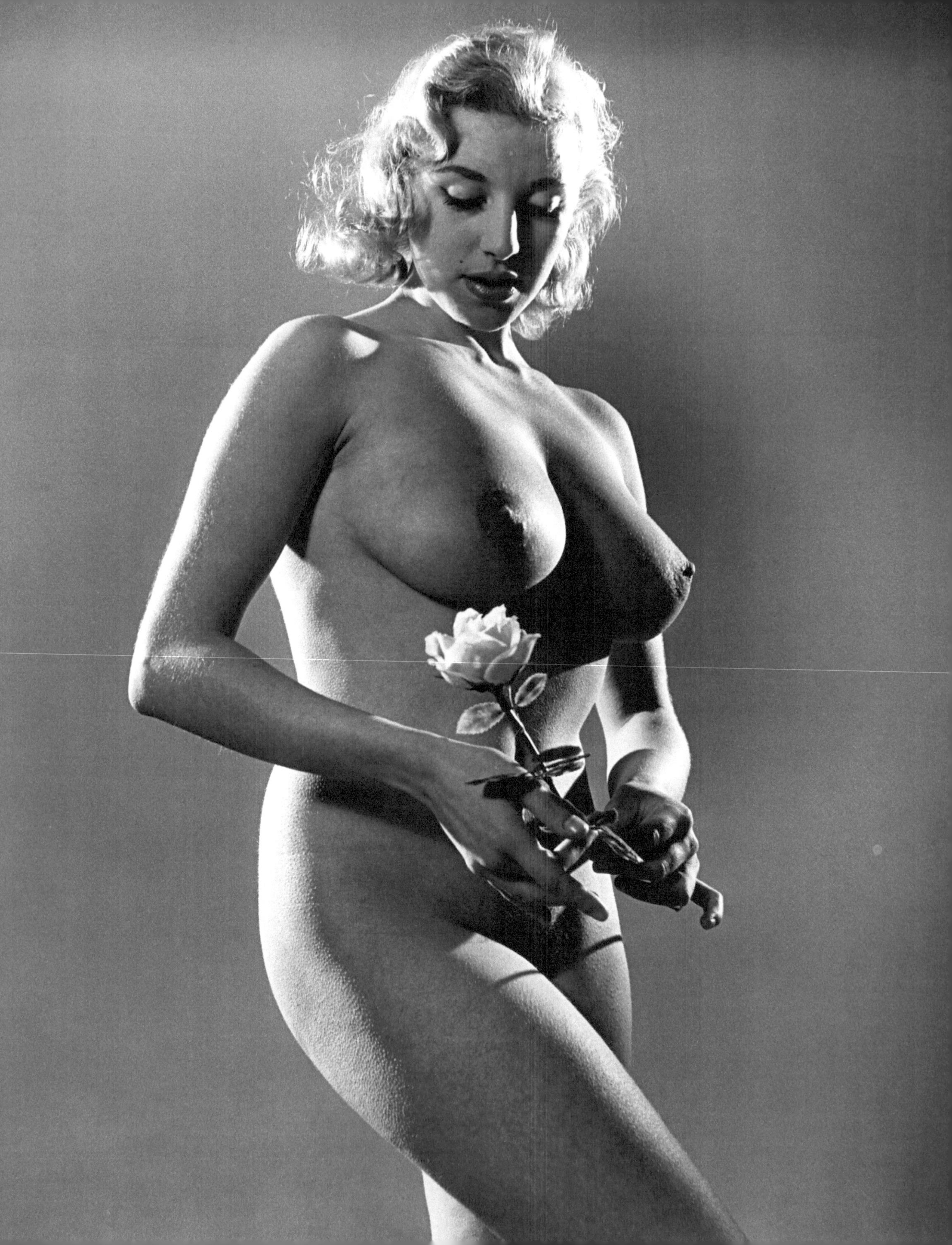

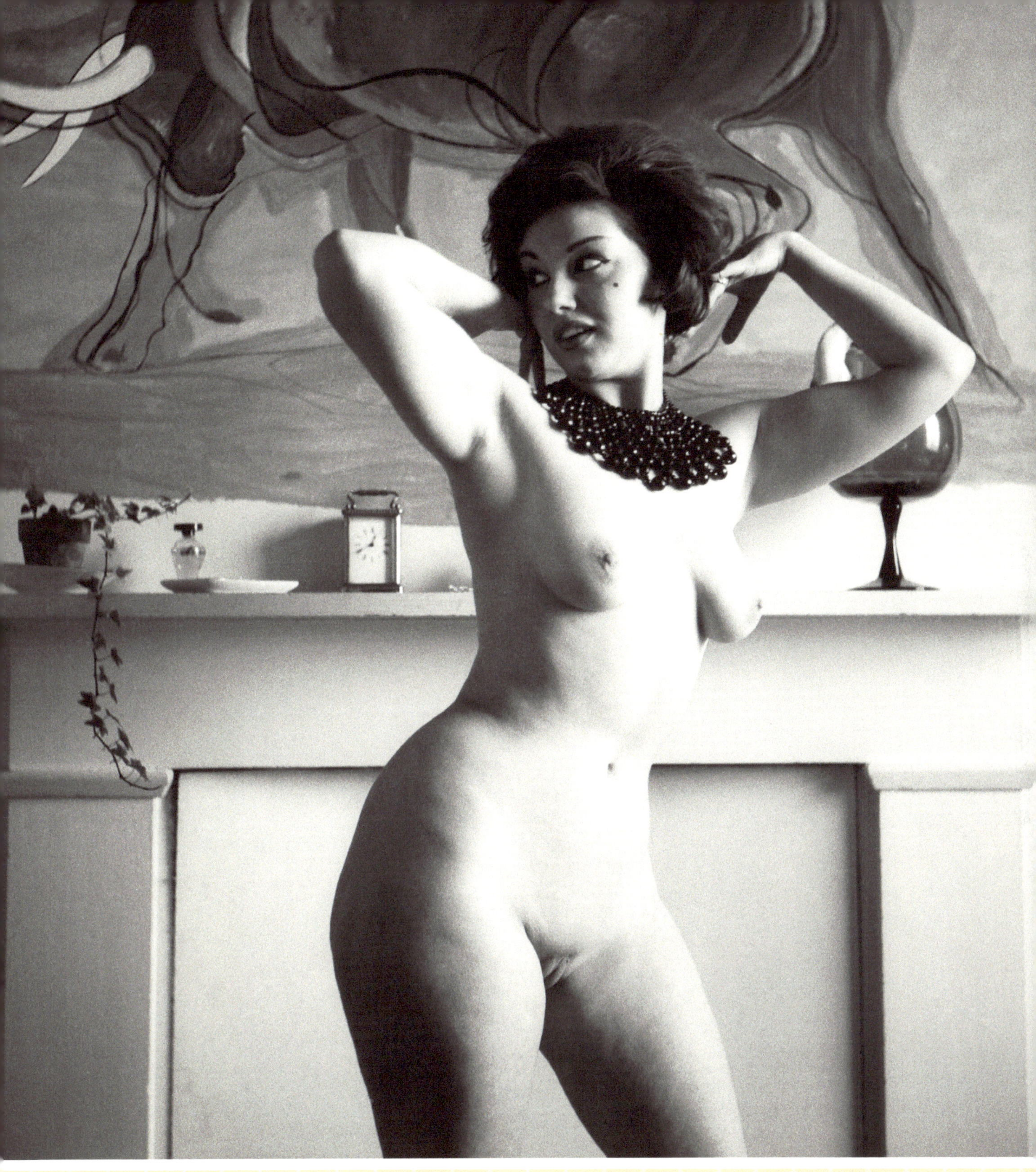

Above: Jackie Aspen.

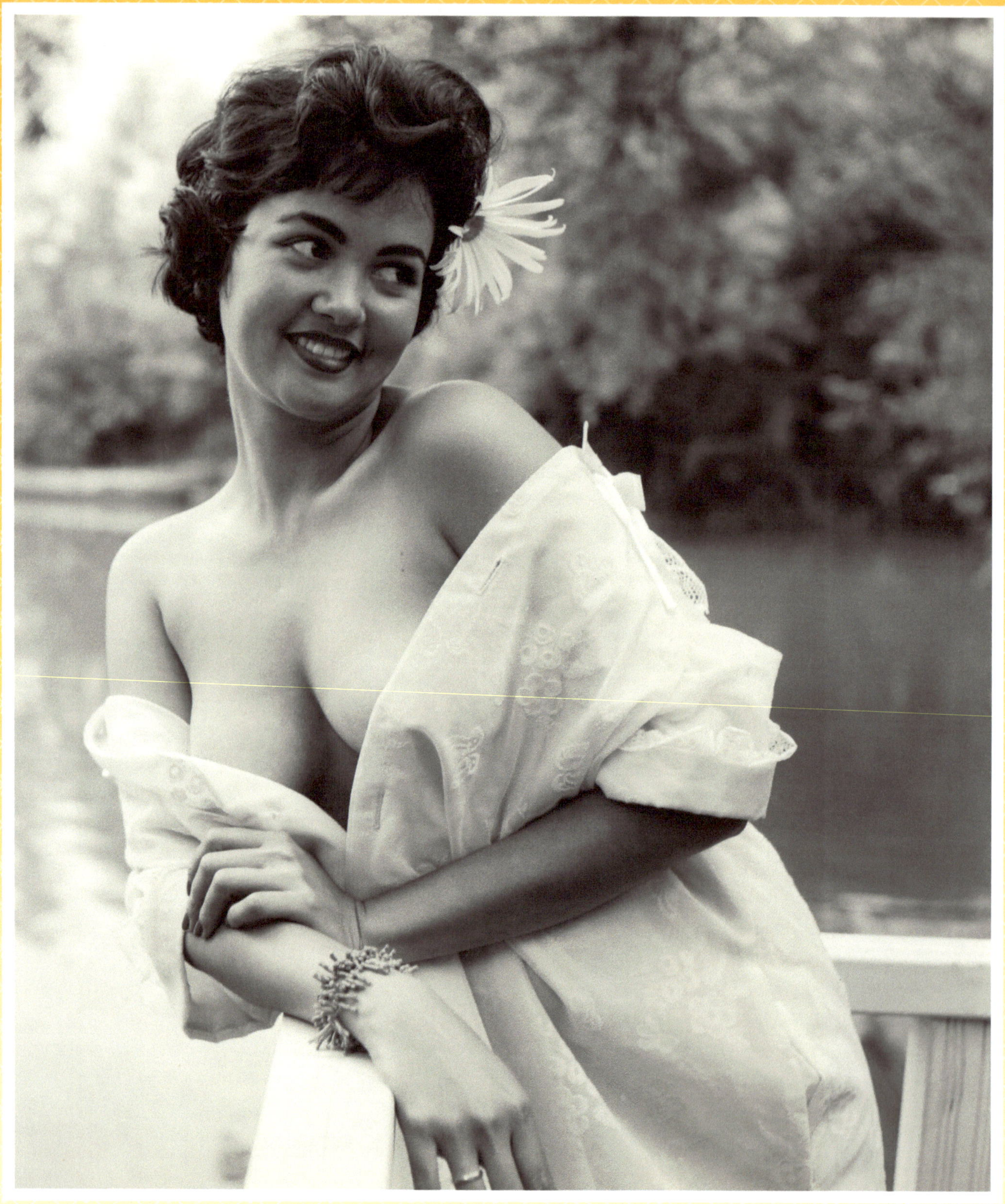

Above: Crystal Dawson. **Opposite:** Ann Walker.

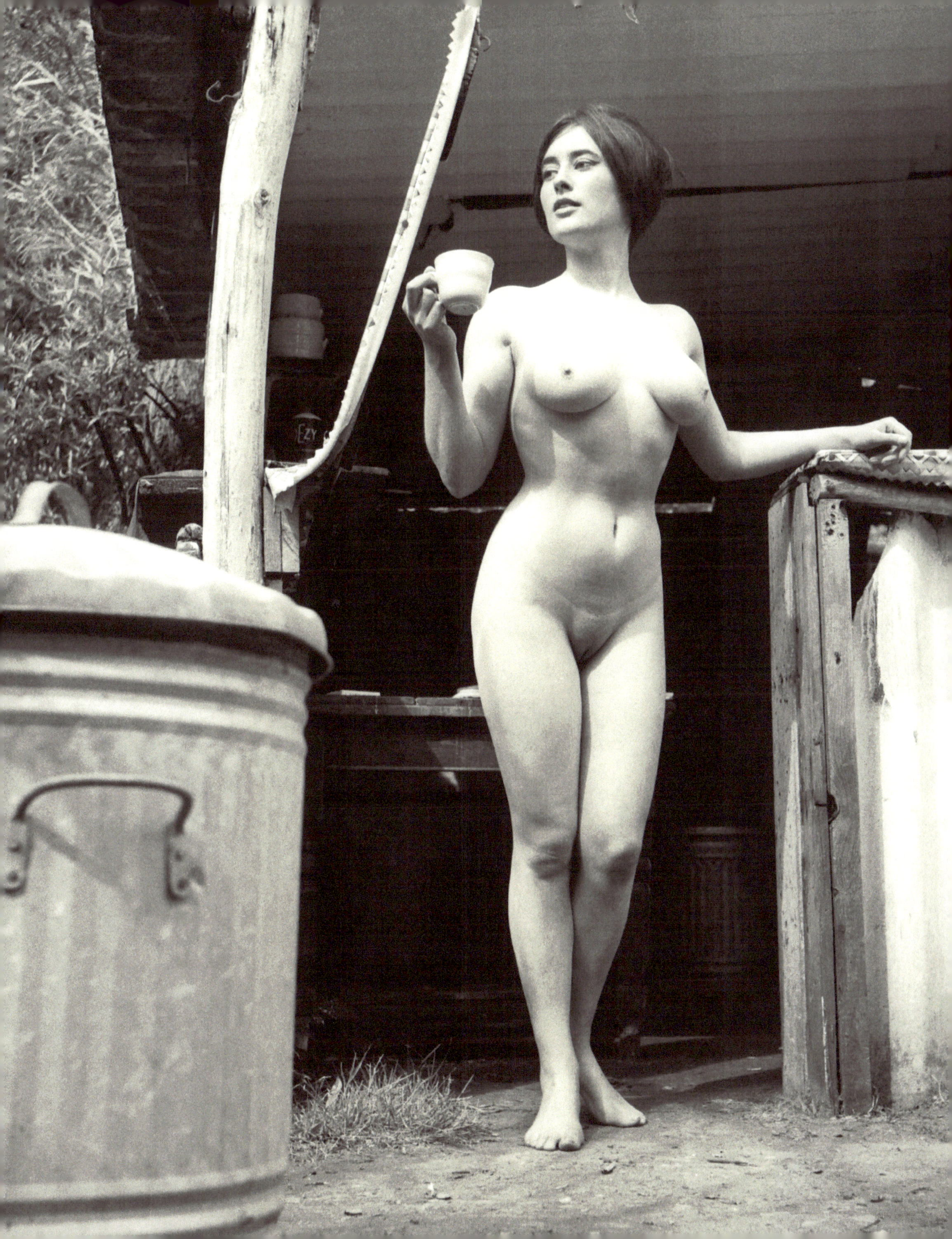

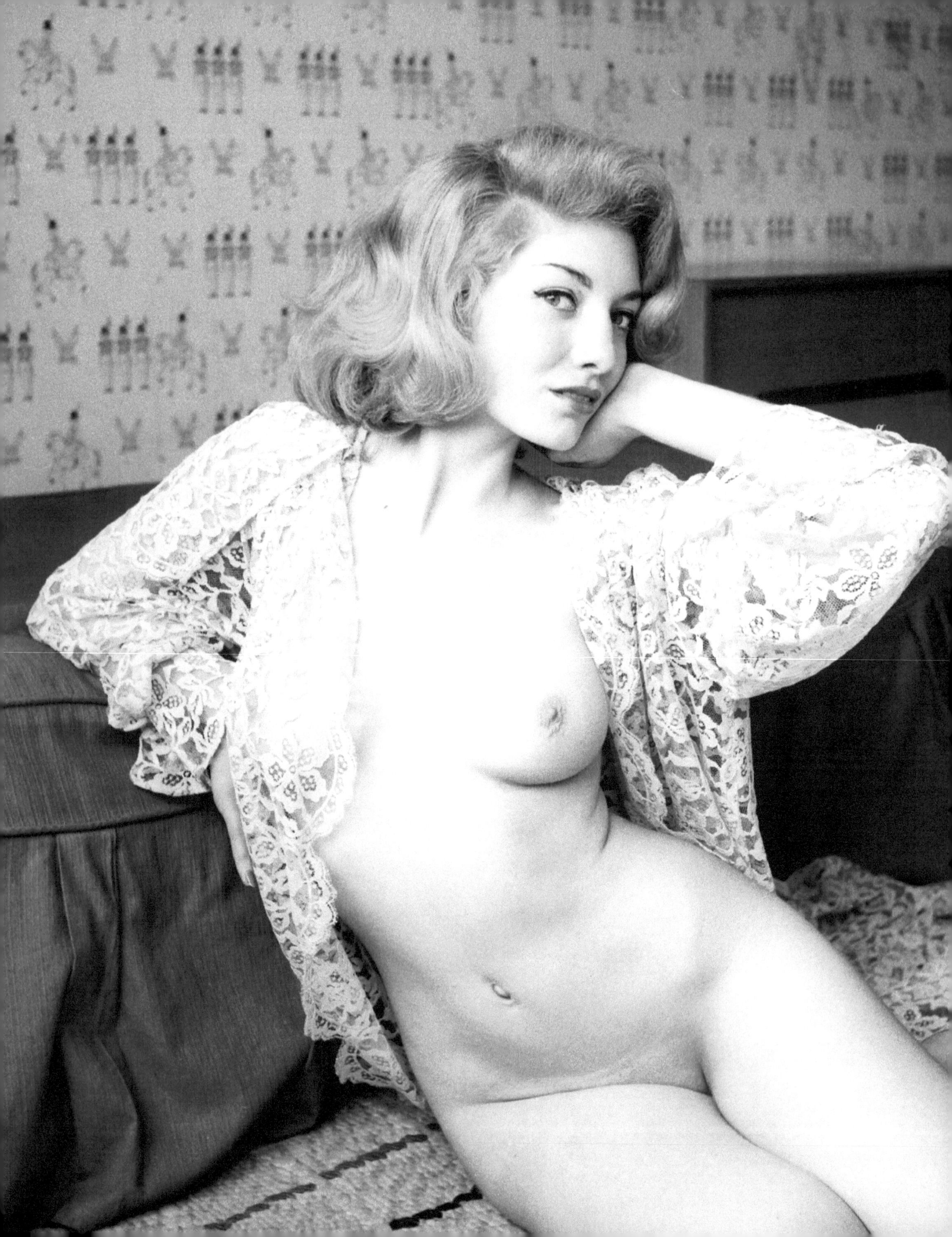

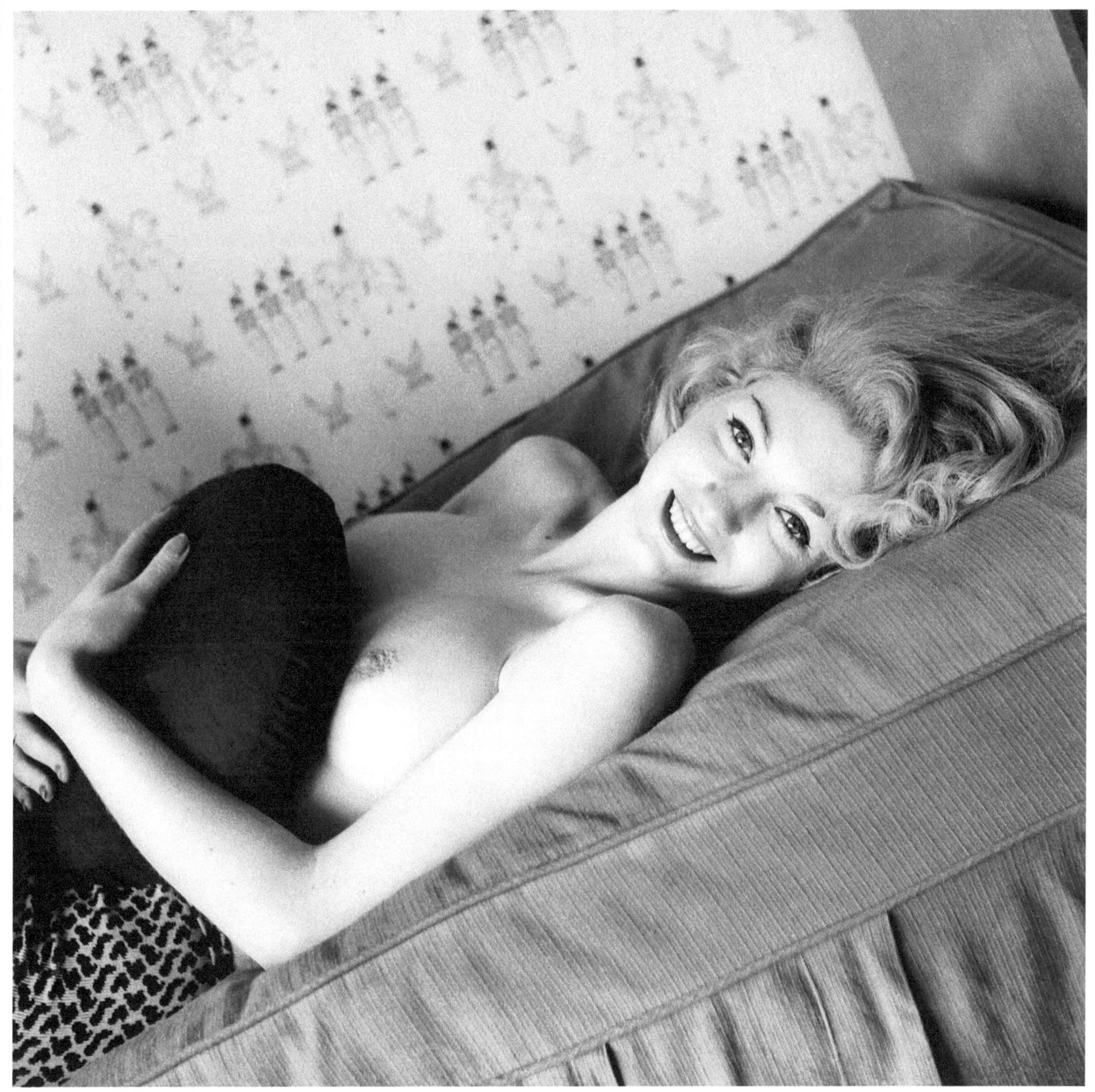

Above and opposite: Anita Martin.

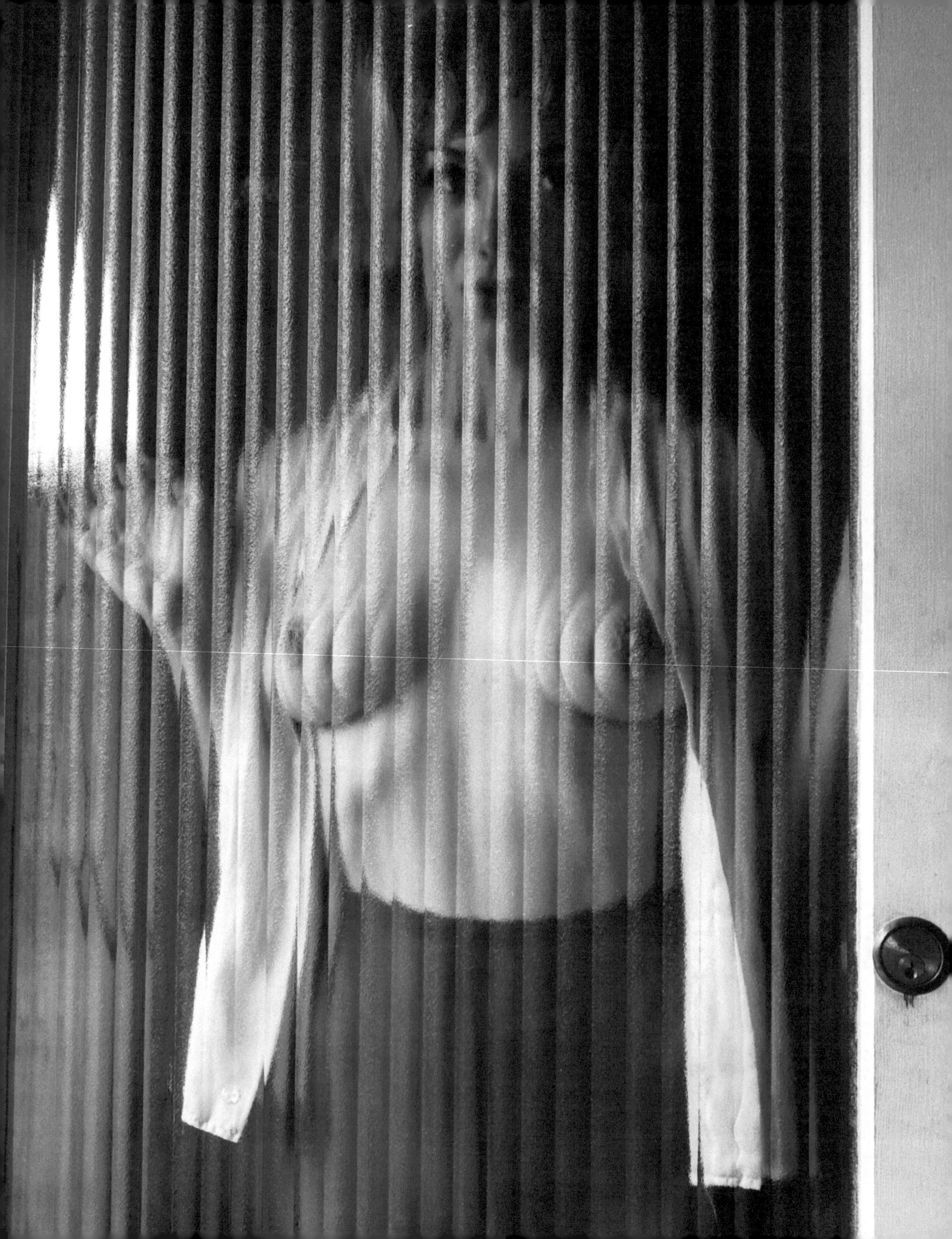

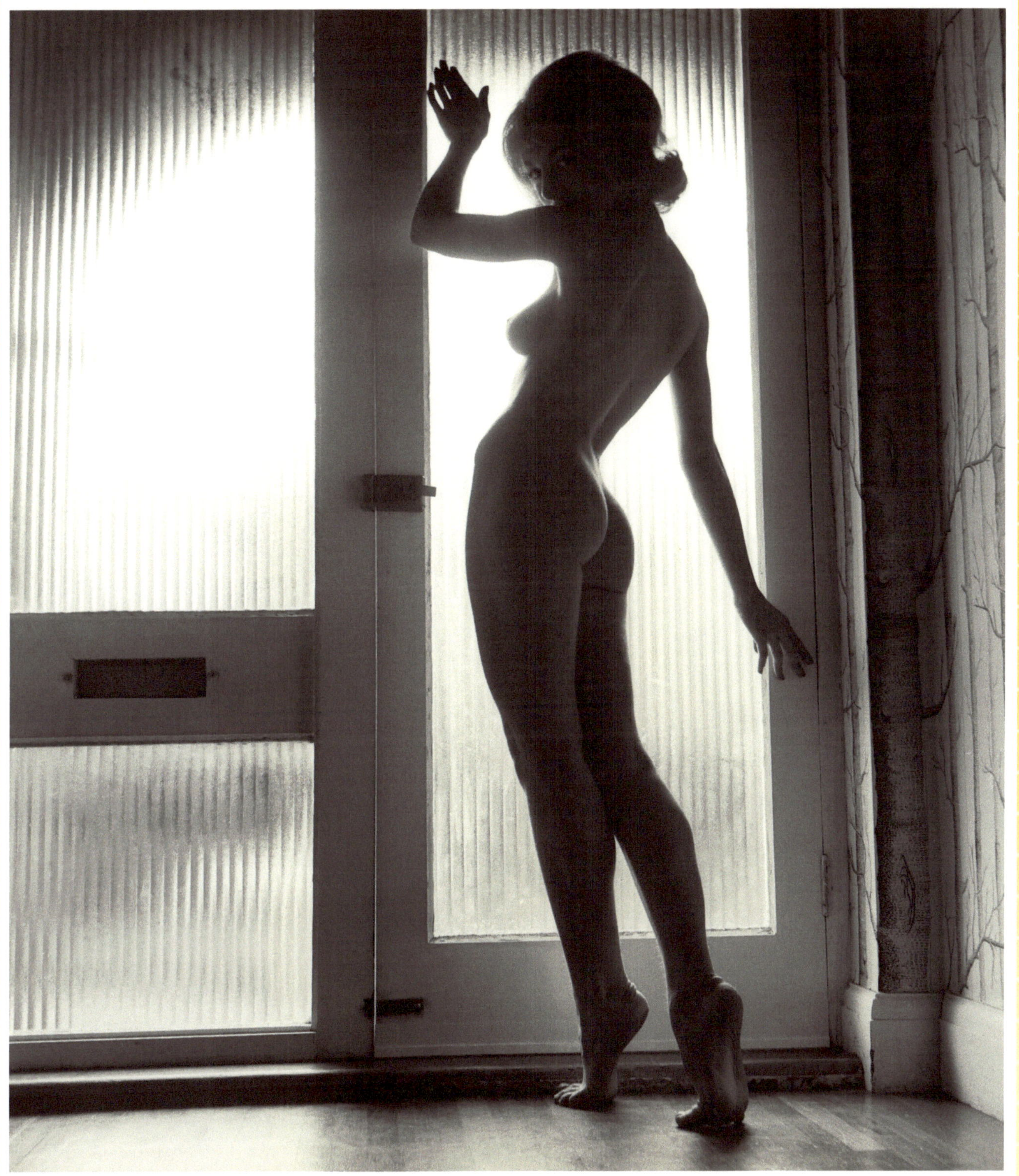

Above and opposite: Anita Martin.

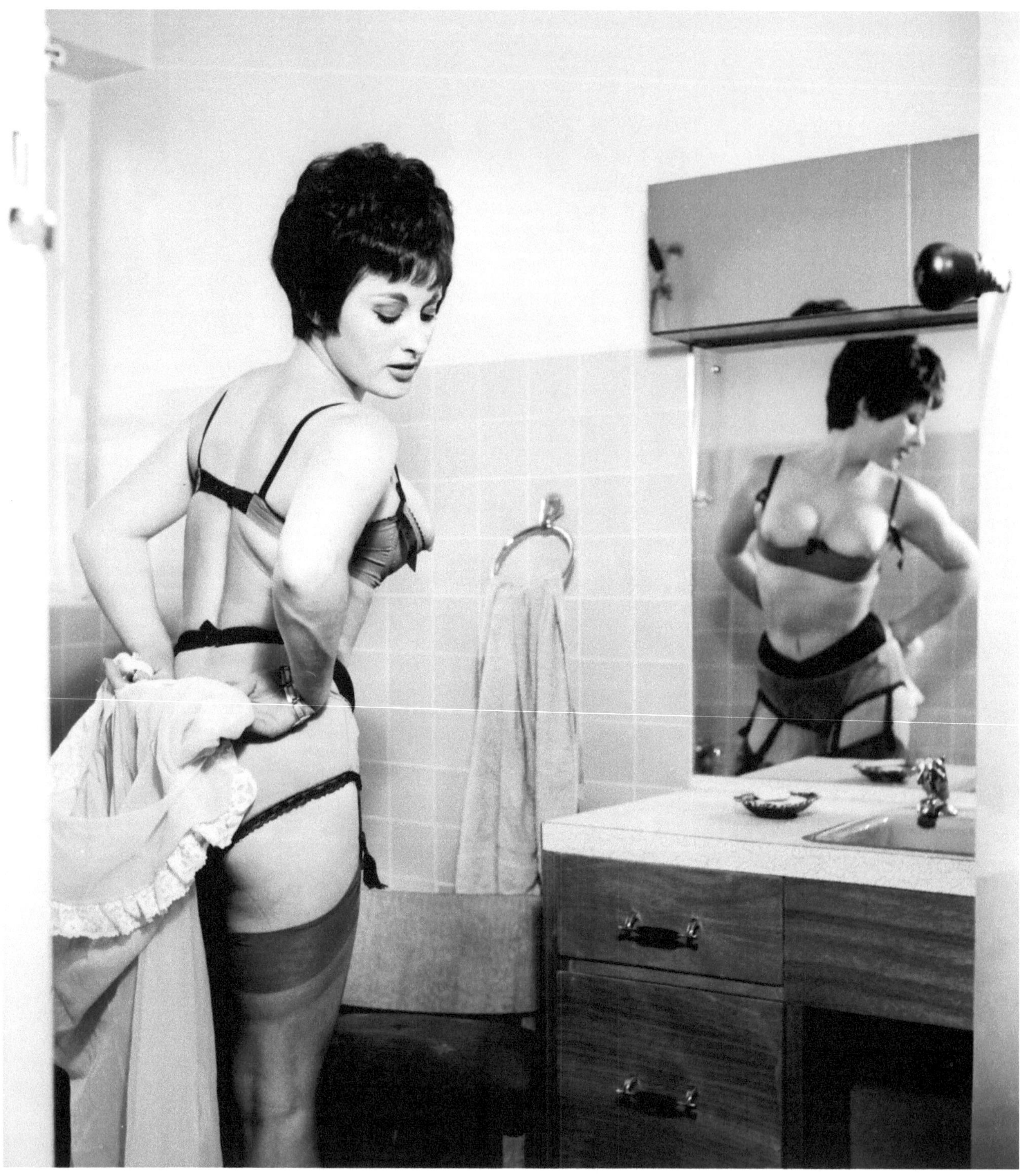

Above: Erna. **Opposite:** June Palmer.

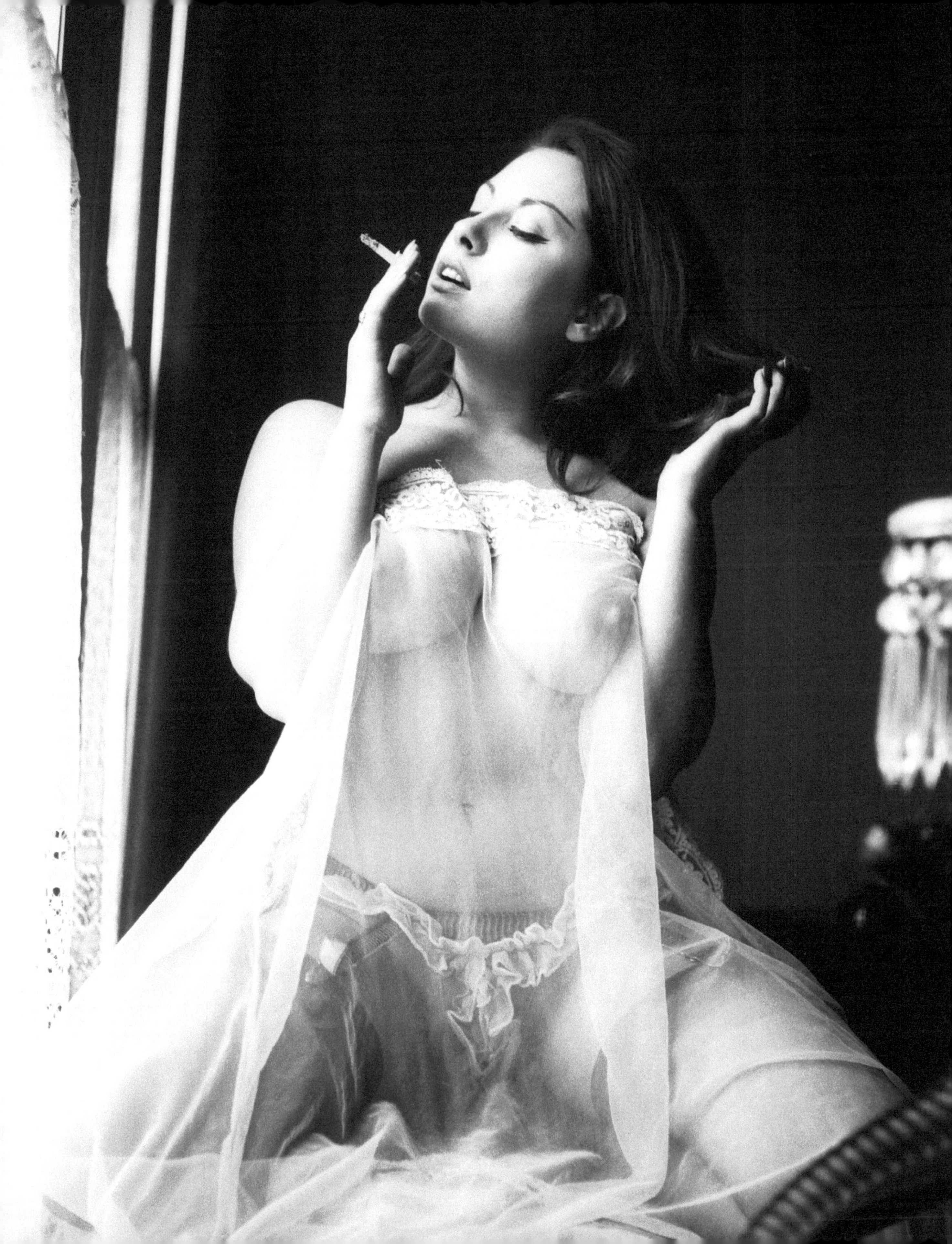

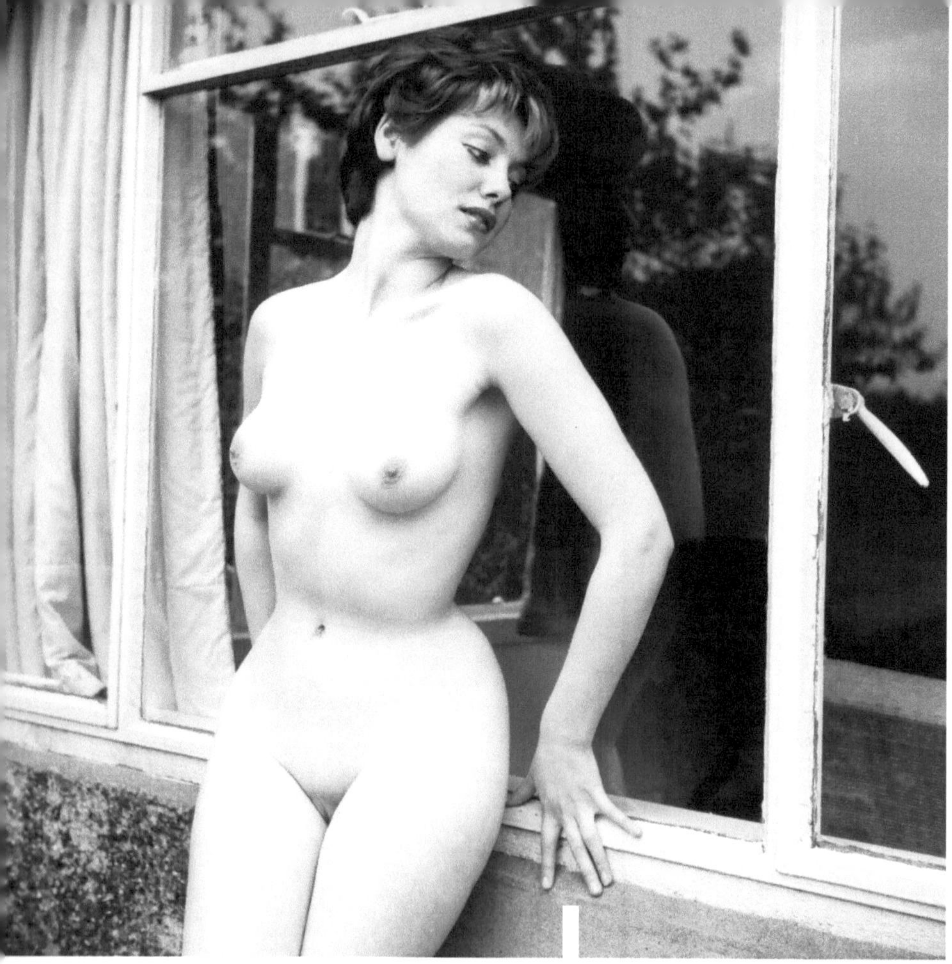

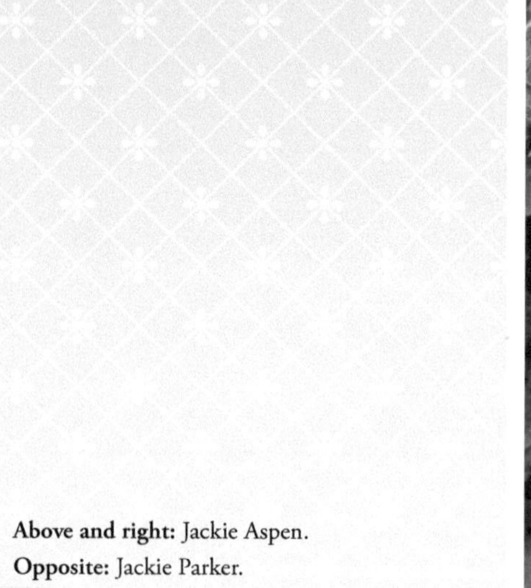

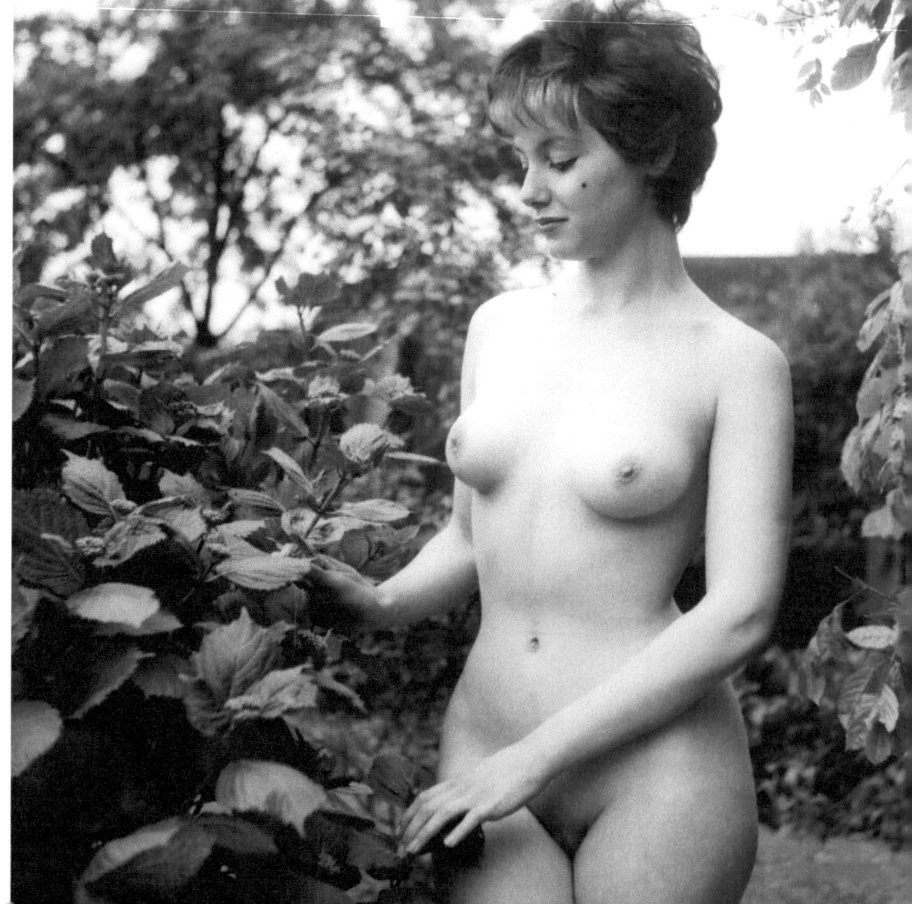

Above and right: Jackie Aspen.
Opposite: Jackie Parker.

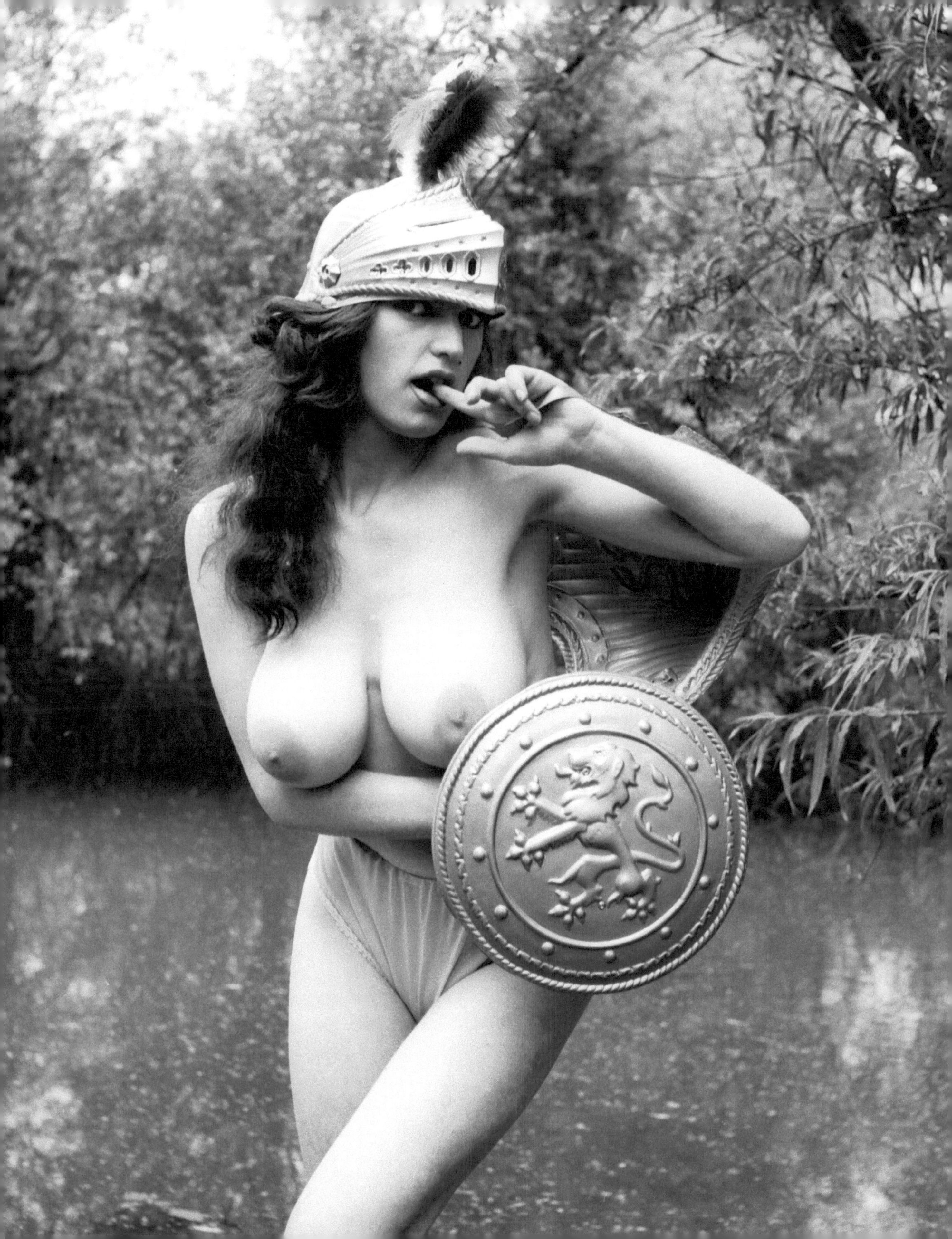

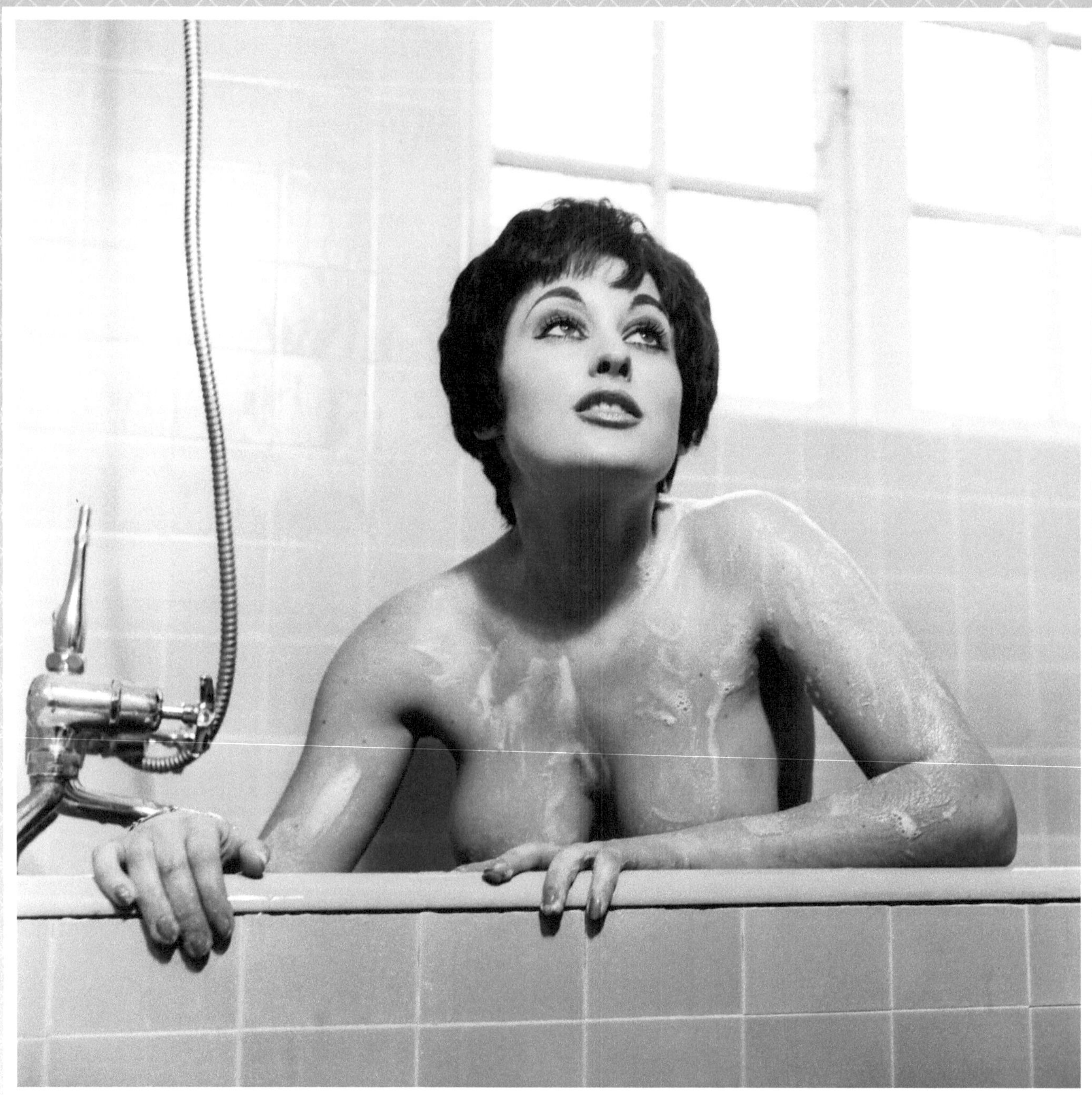

Above and opposite: Erna.

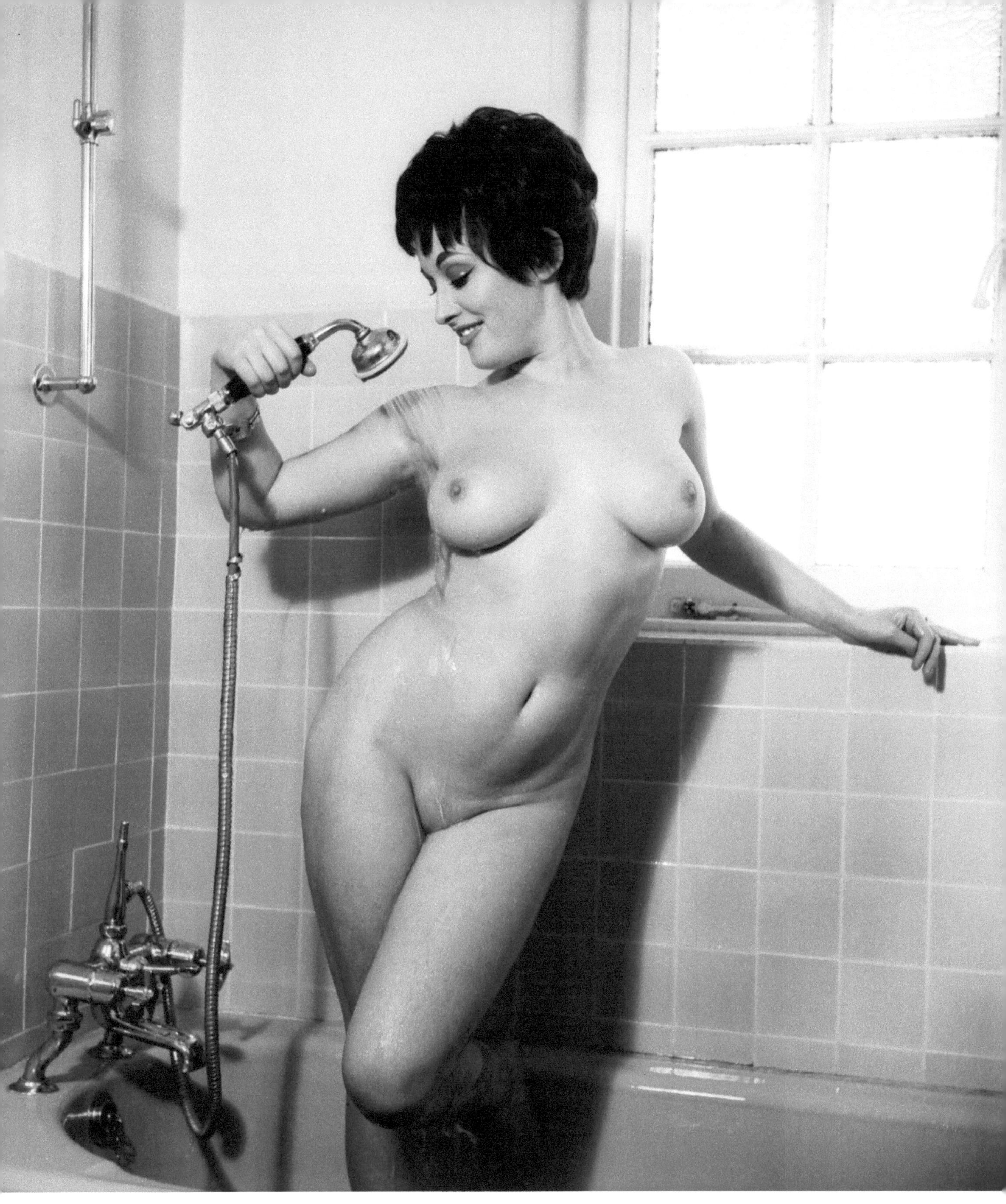

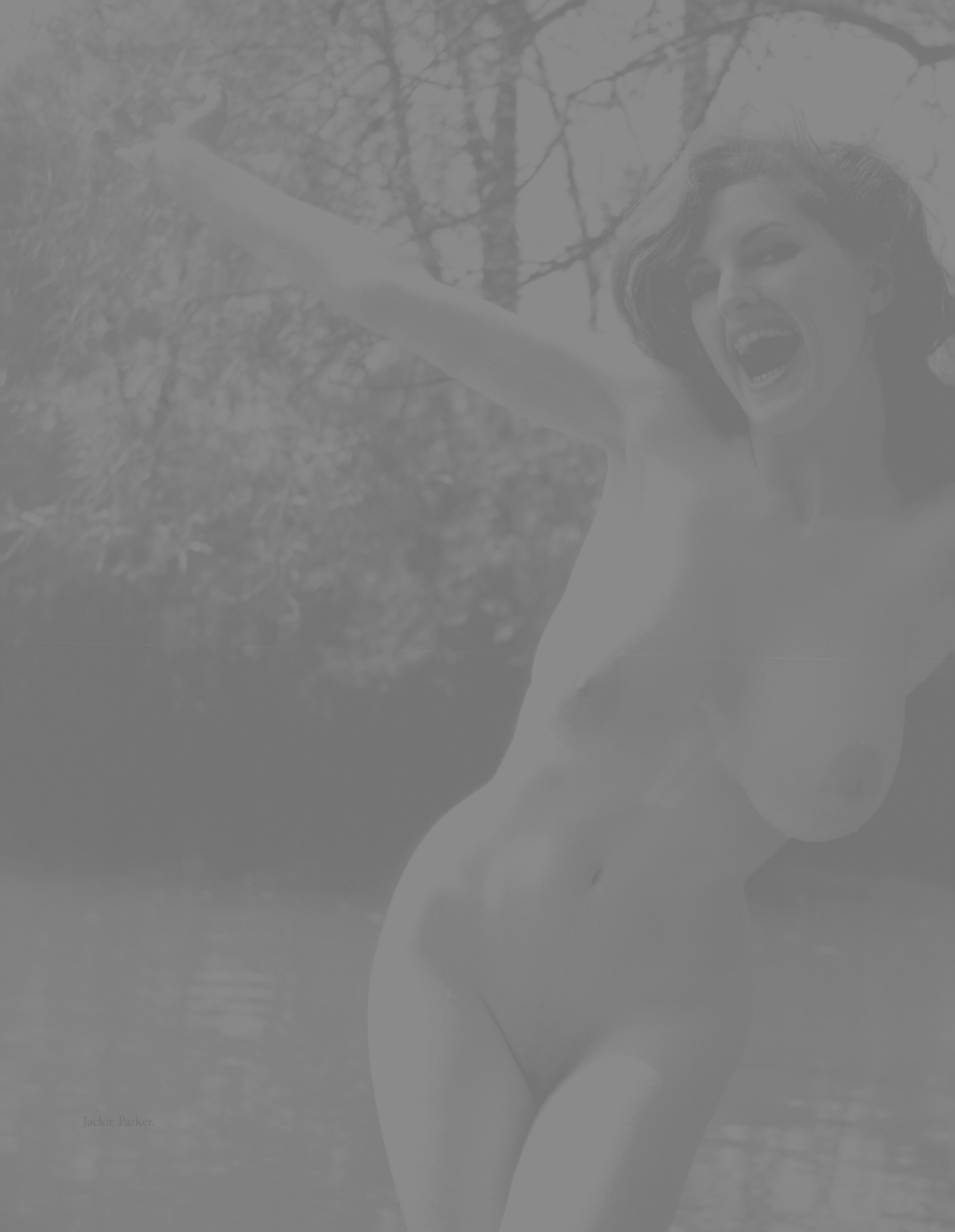

Jackie Parker.

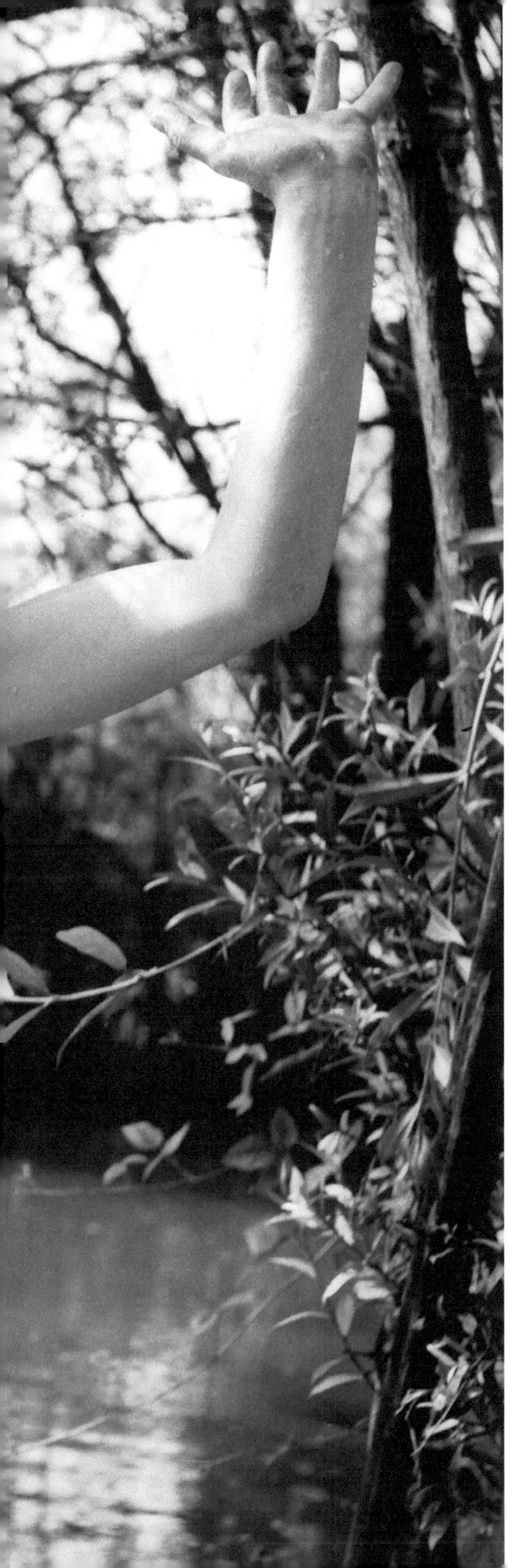

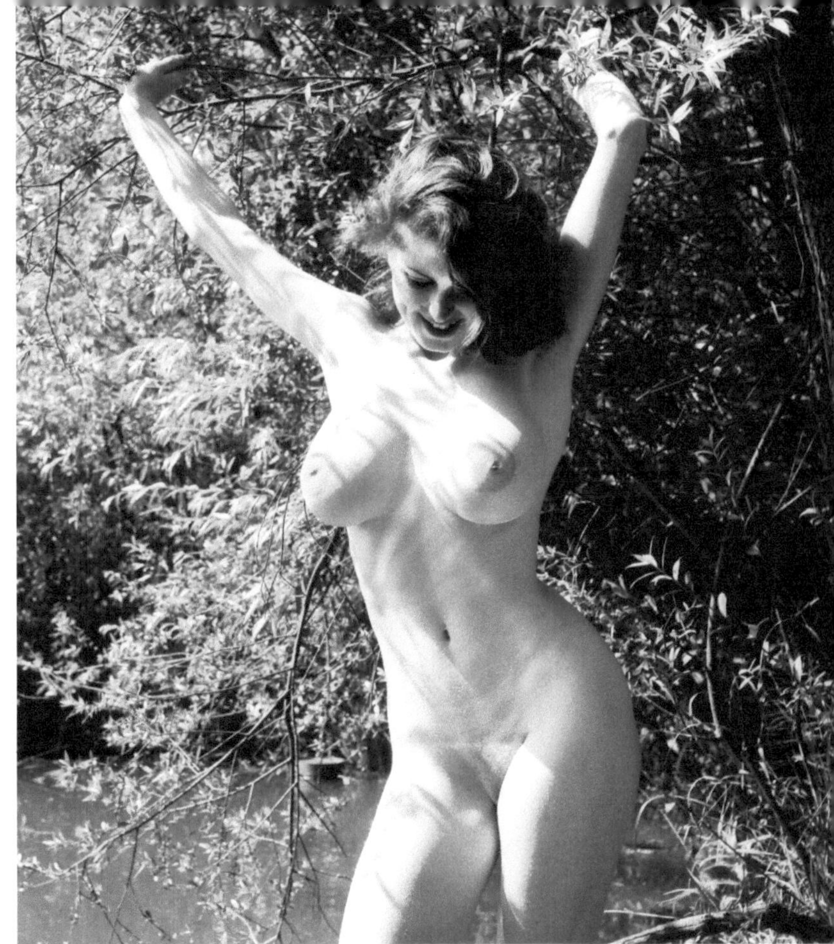

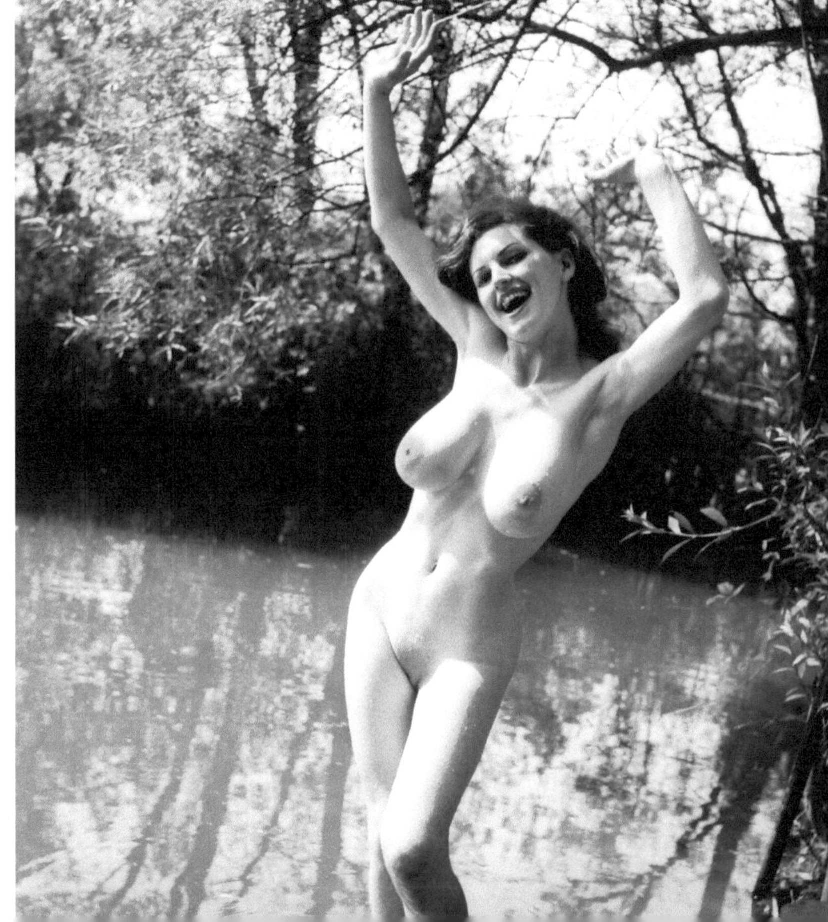

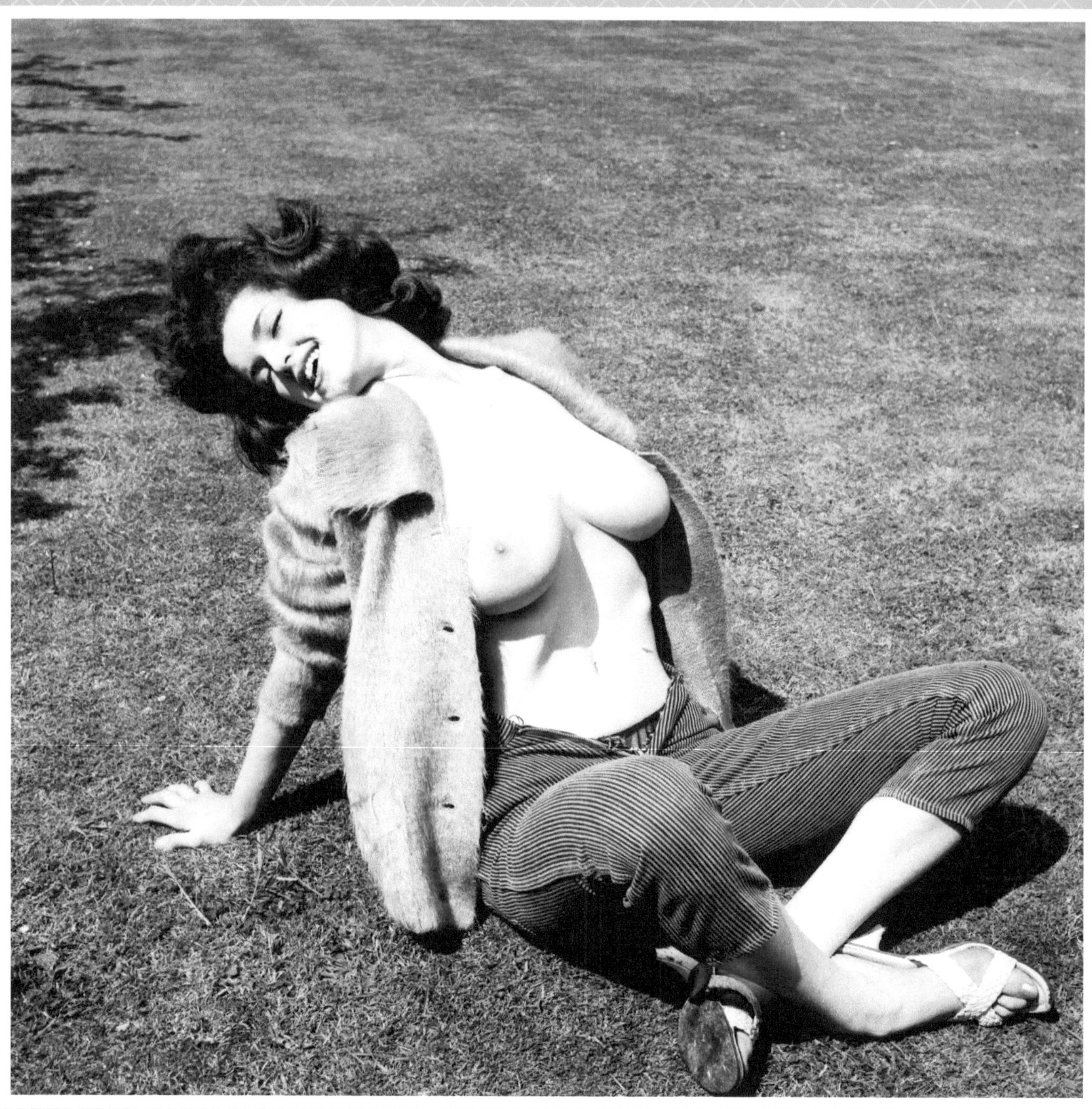

Above and opposite: Jackie Parker.

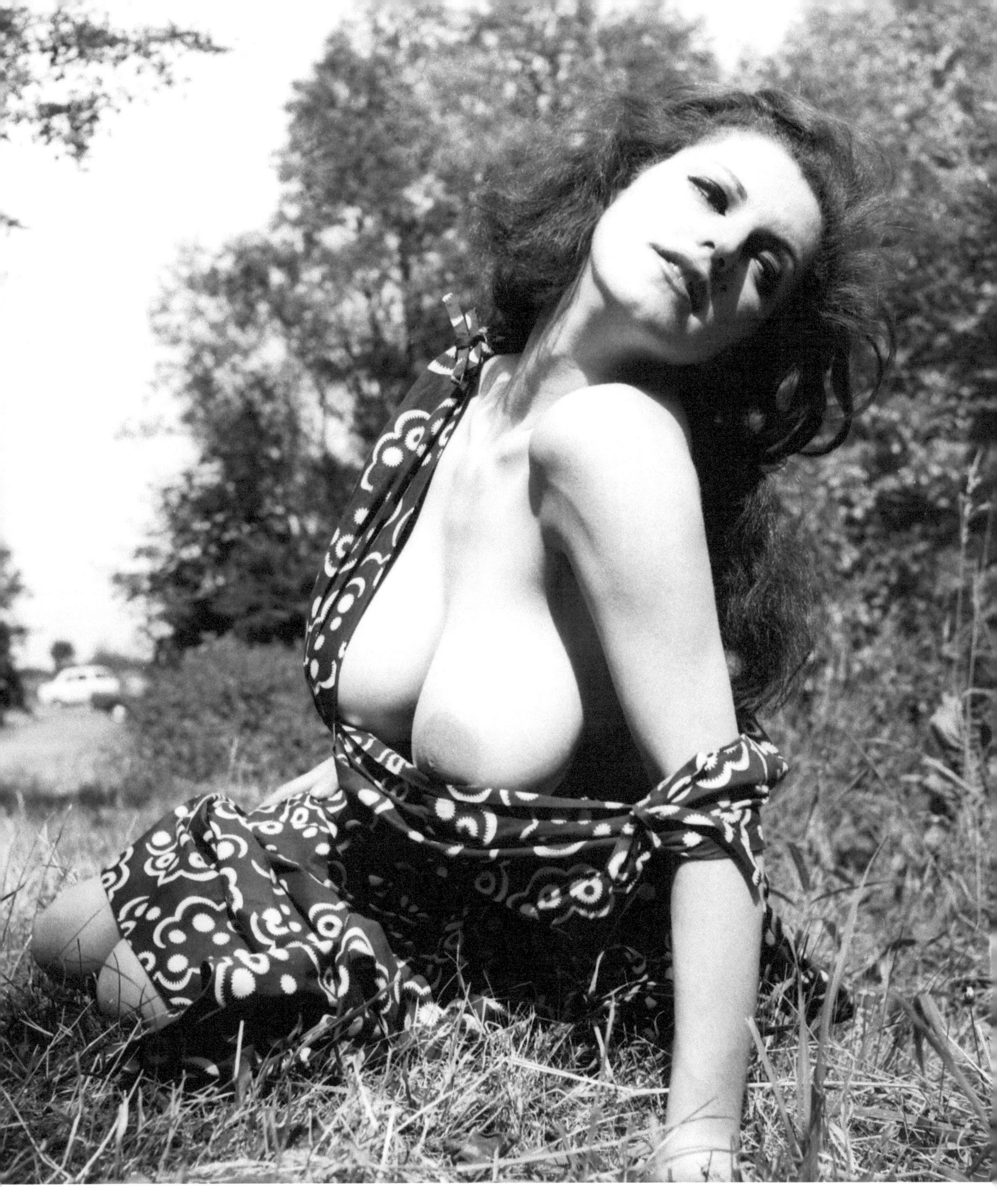

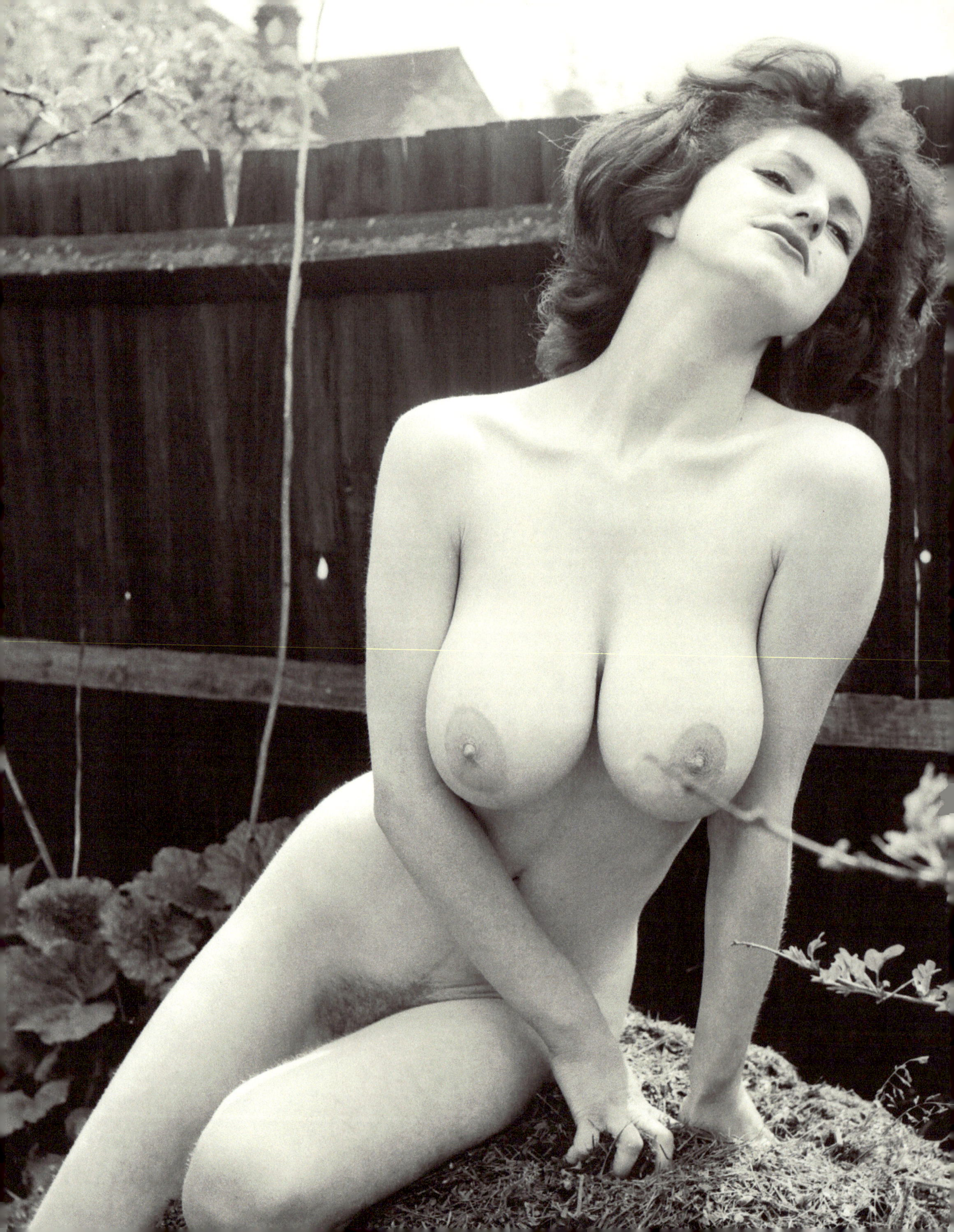

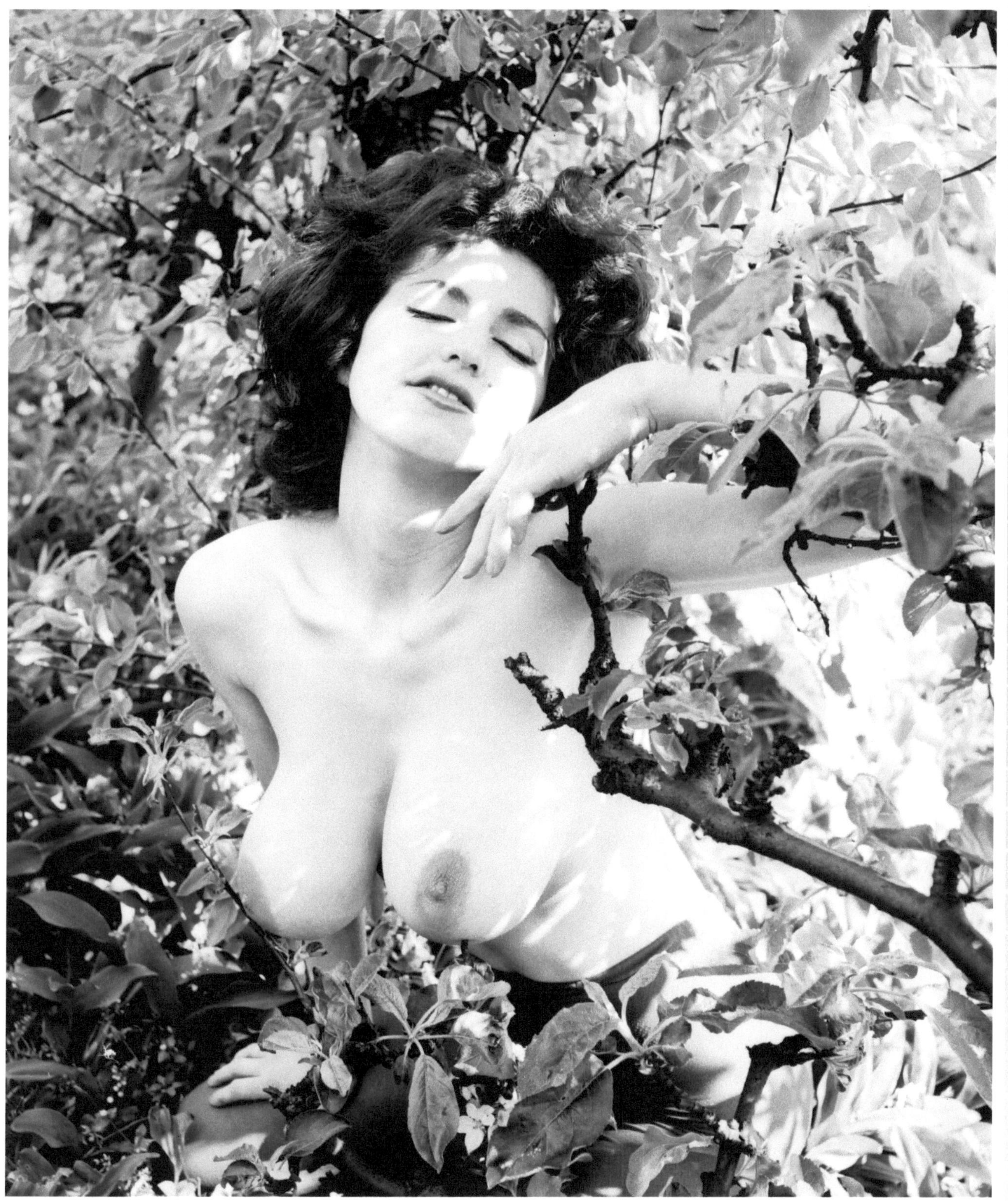

Above and opposite: Jackie Parker.

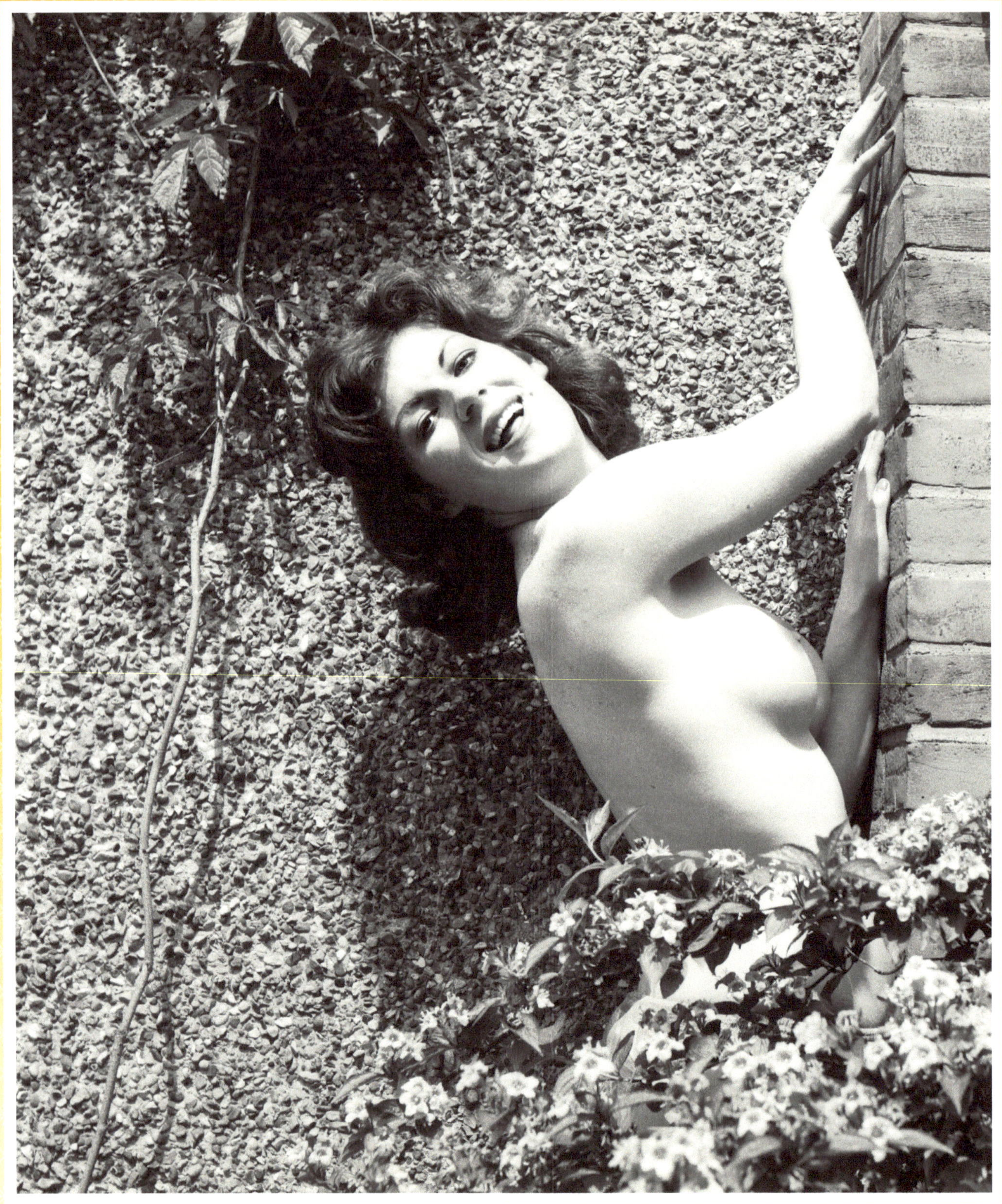

Above: Maria Clarence. **Opposite:** Jane Mathews.

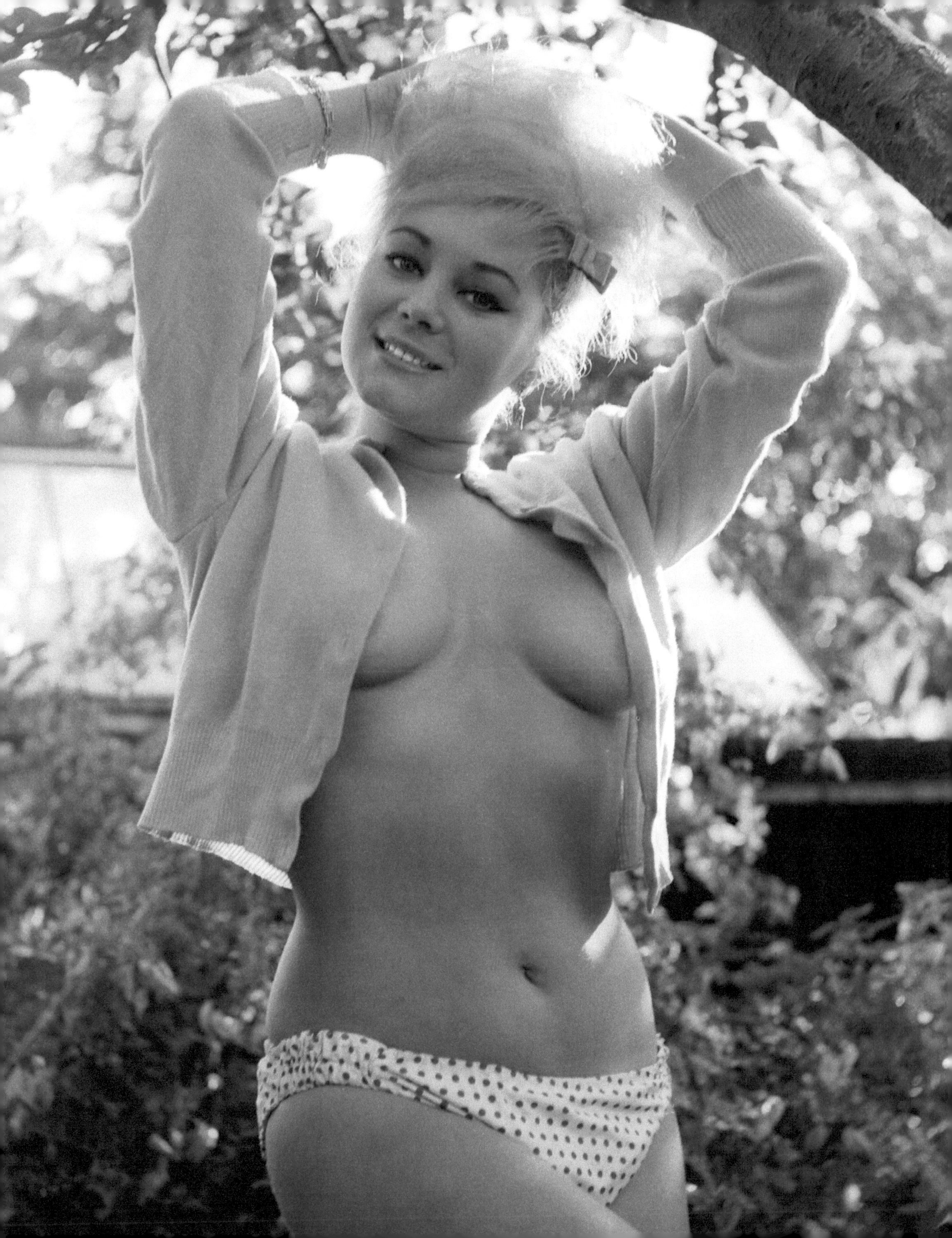

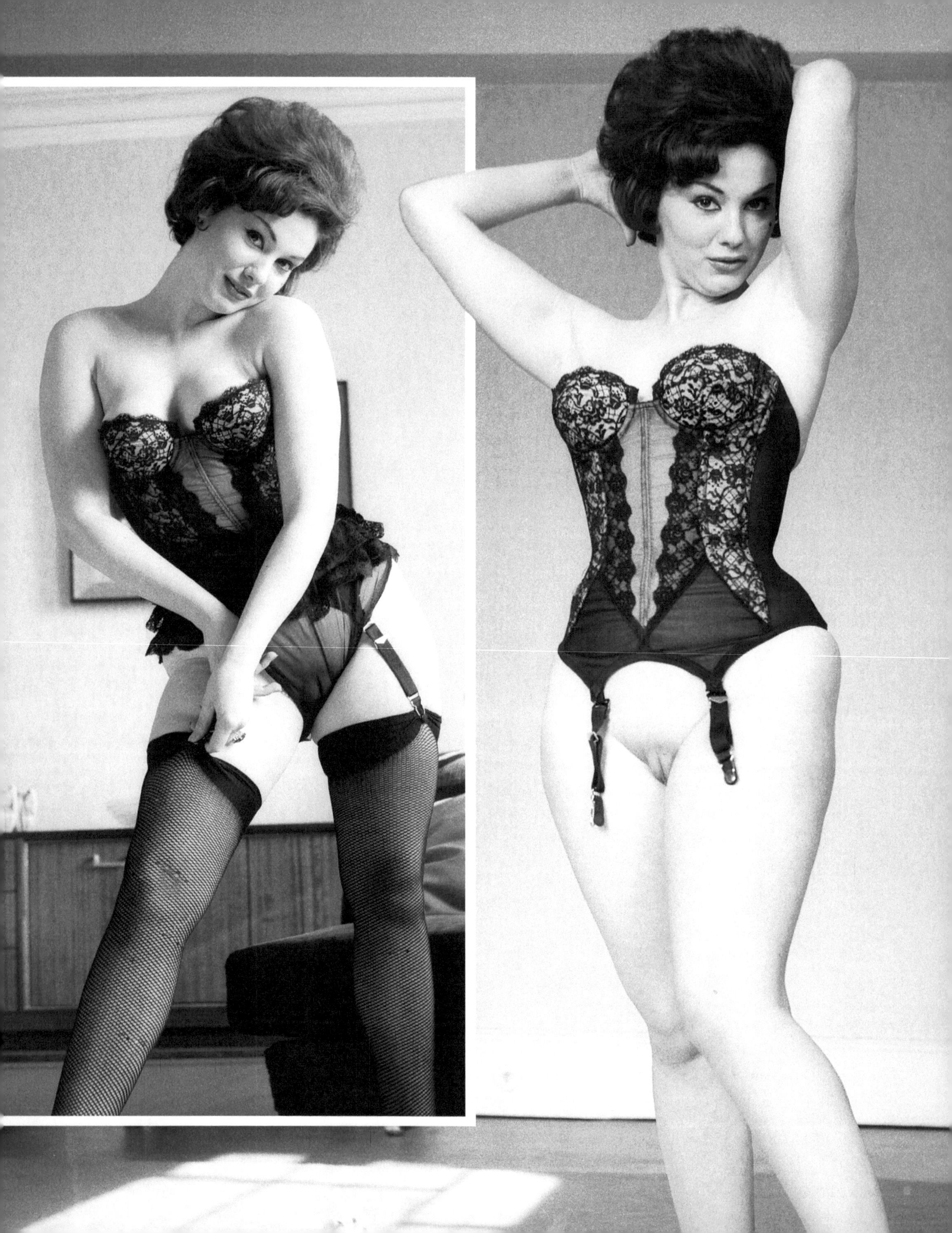

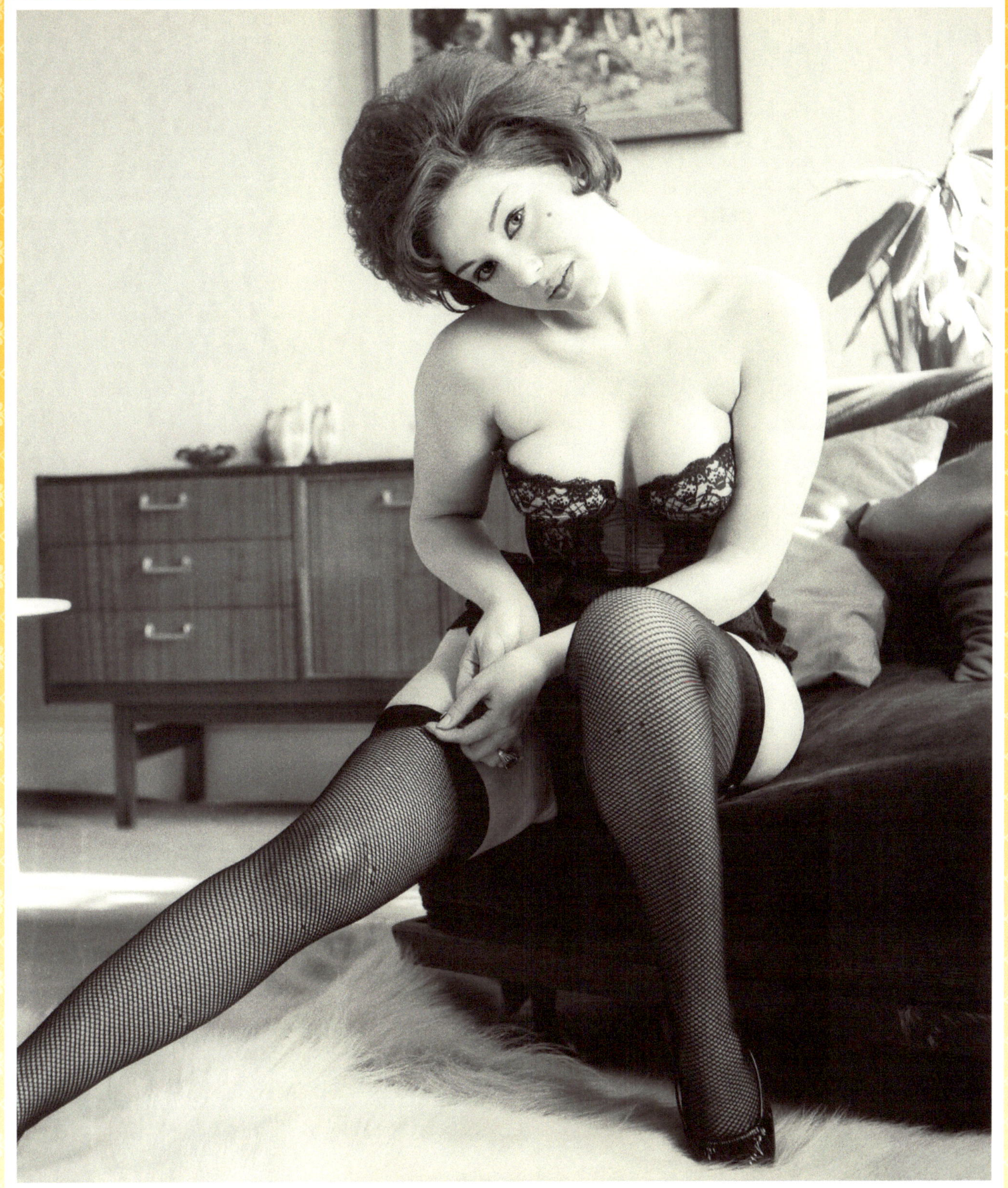

Above and opposite: Jackie Aspen.

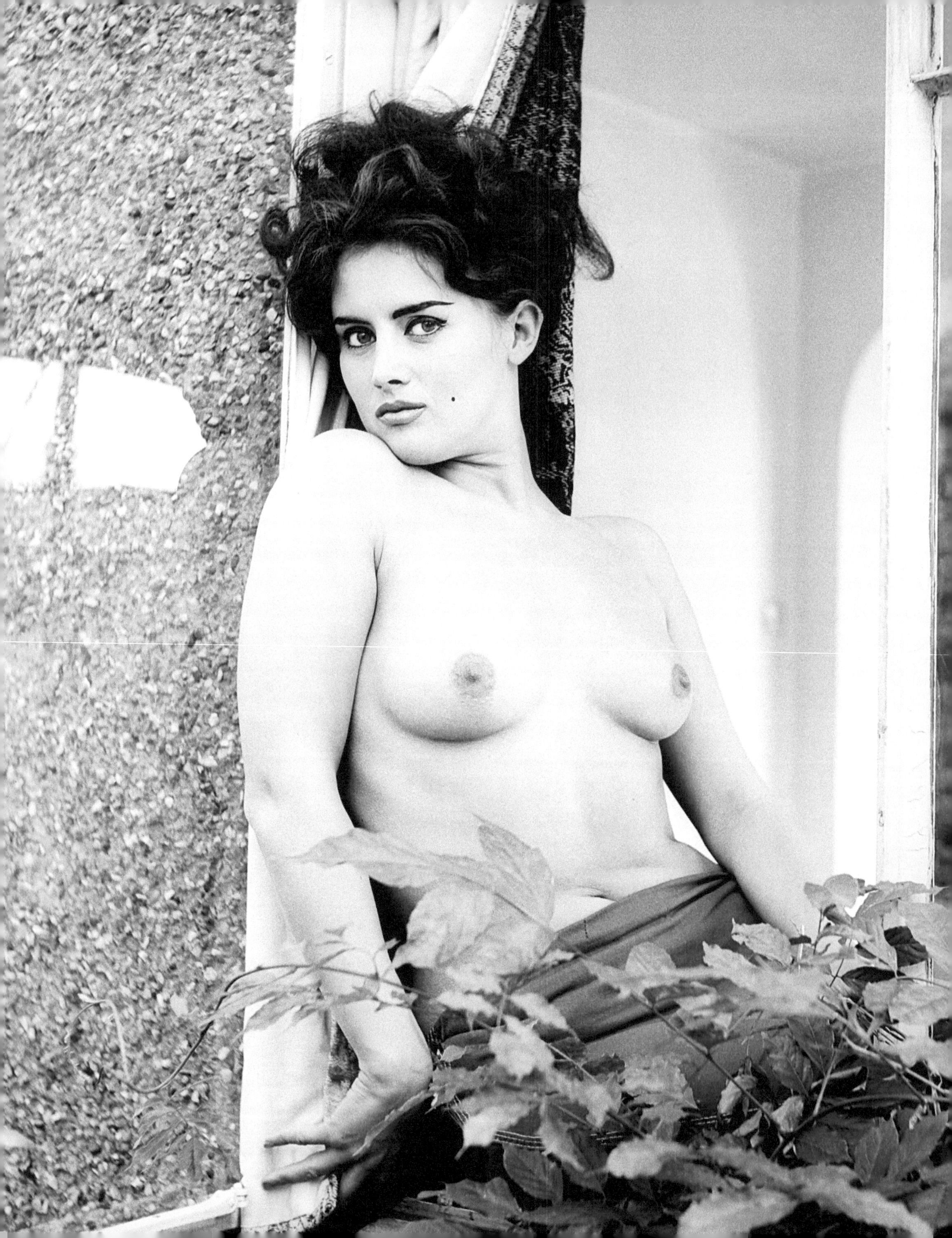

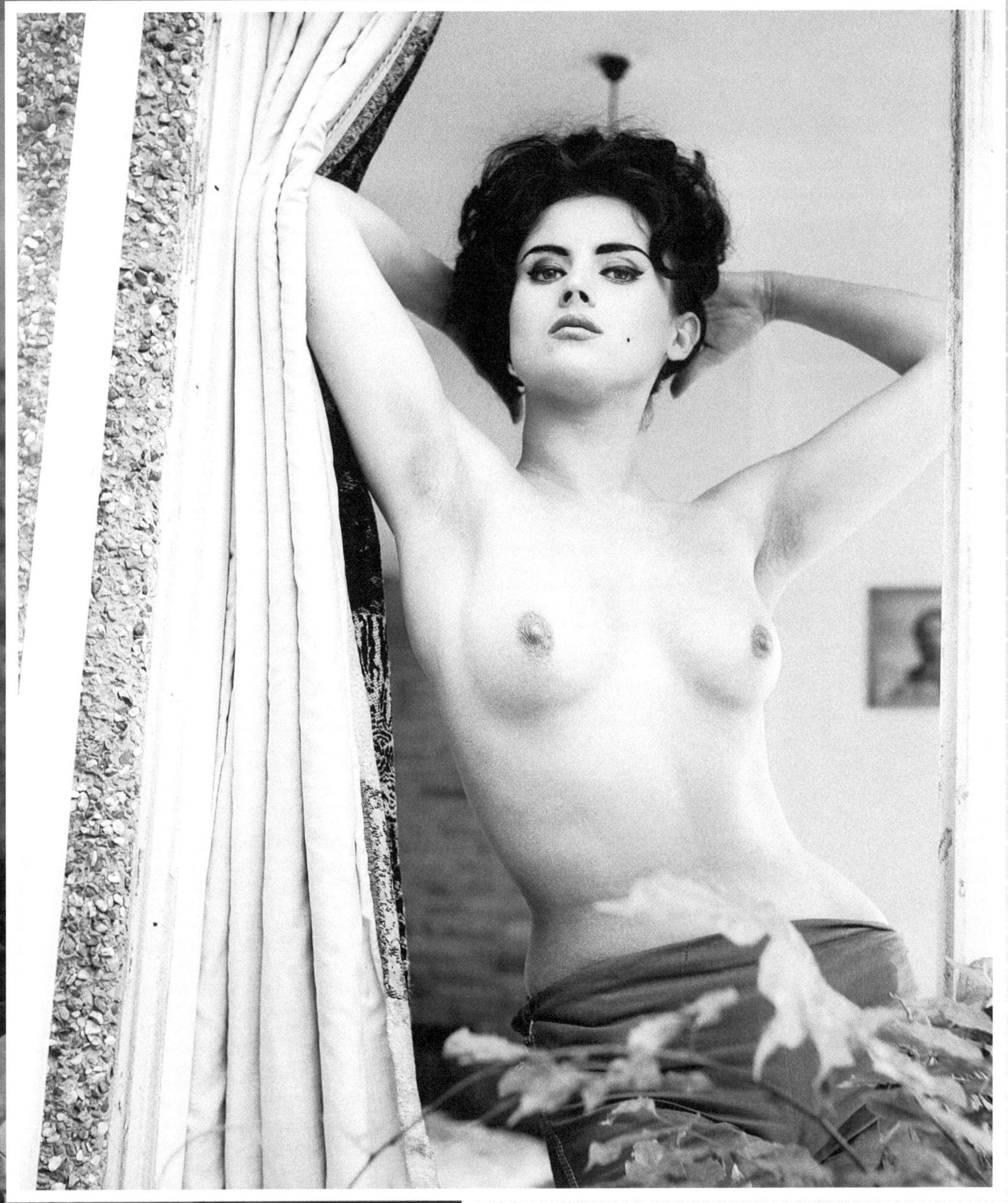

Above and opposite: Sophie Dawn.

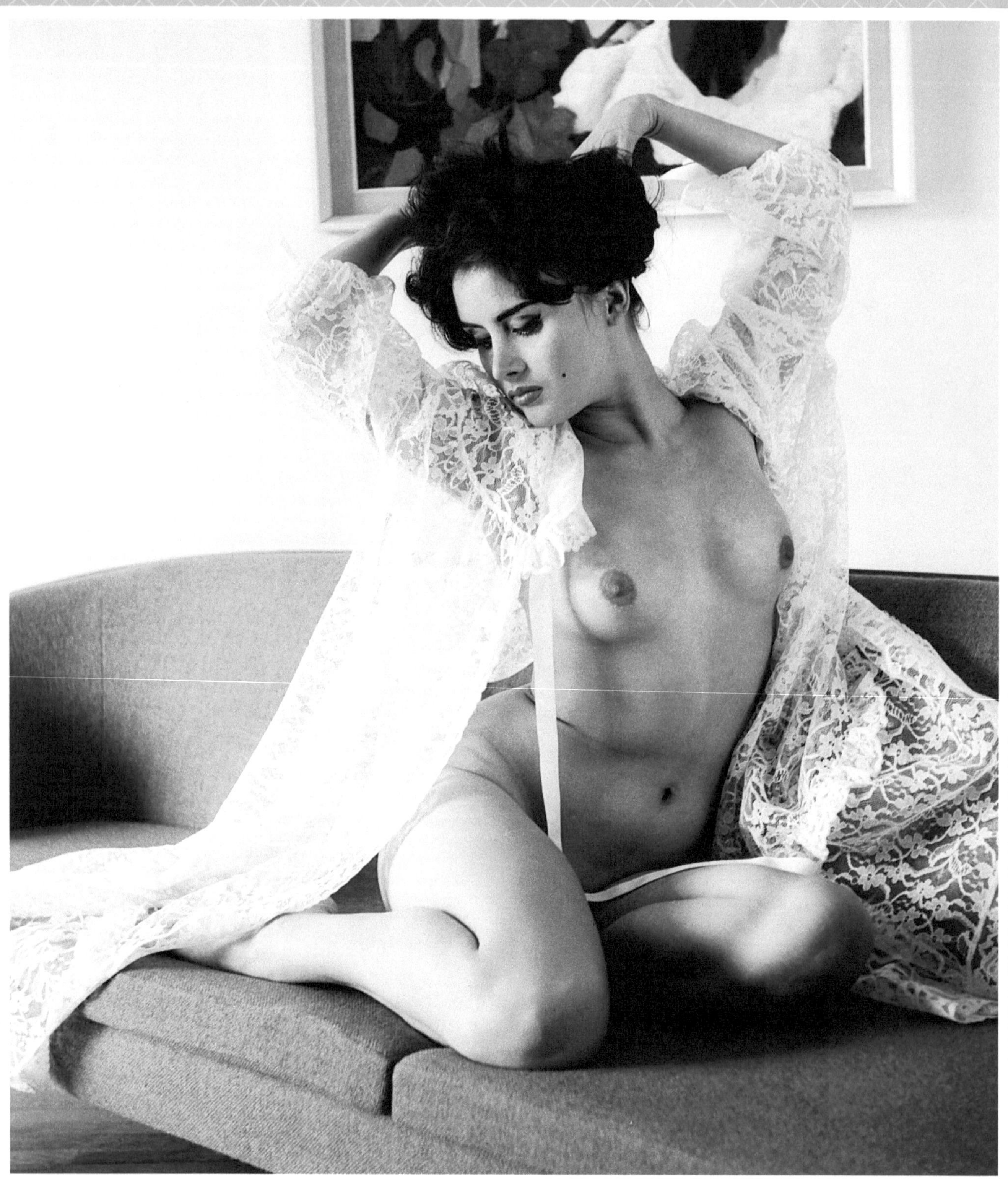

Above and opposite: Sophie Dawn.

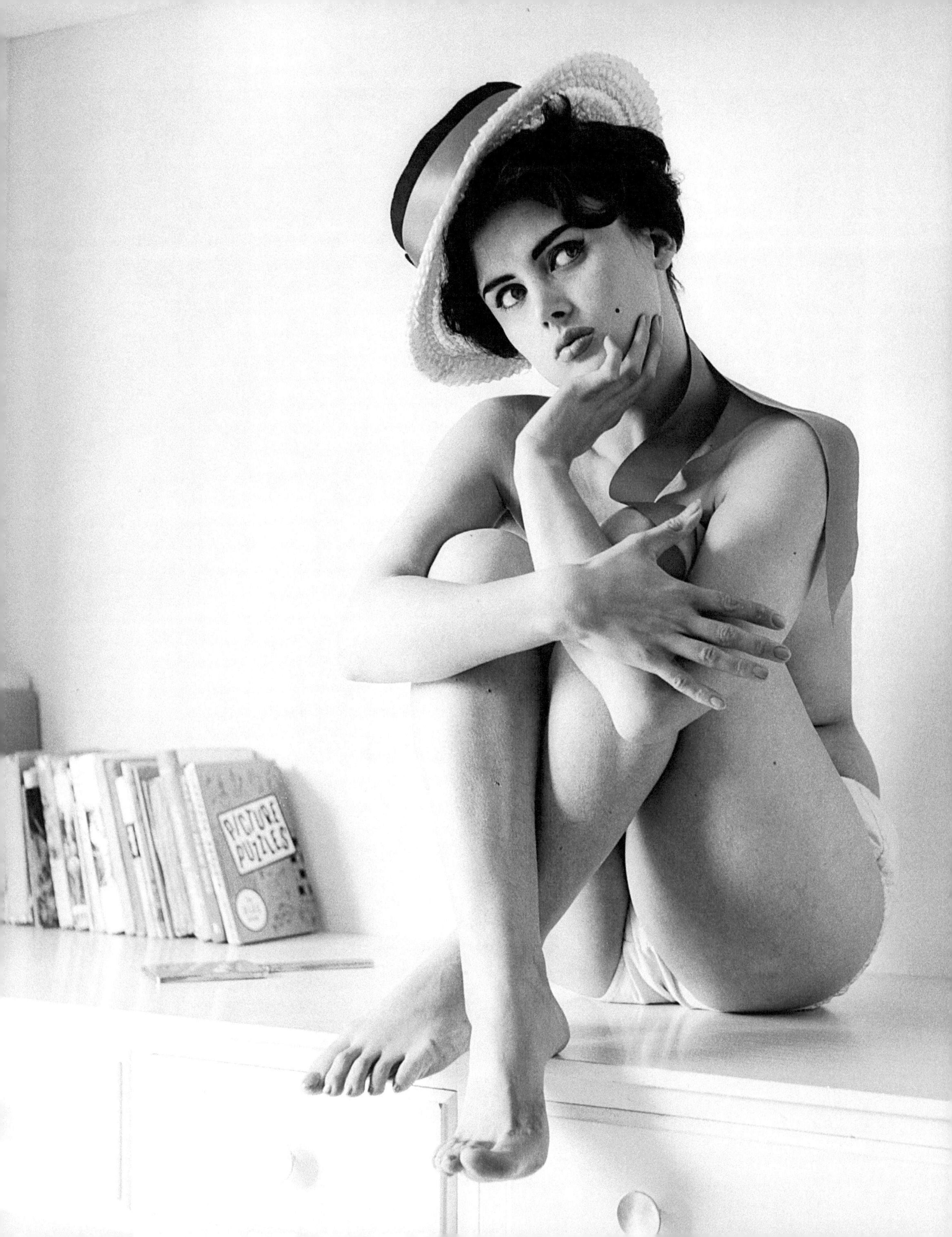

PICTURE
PUZZLES

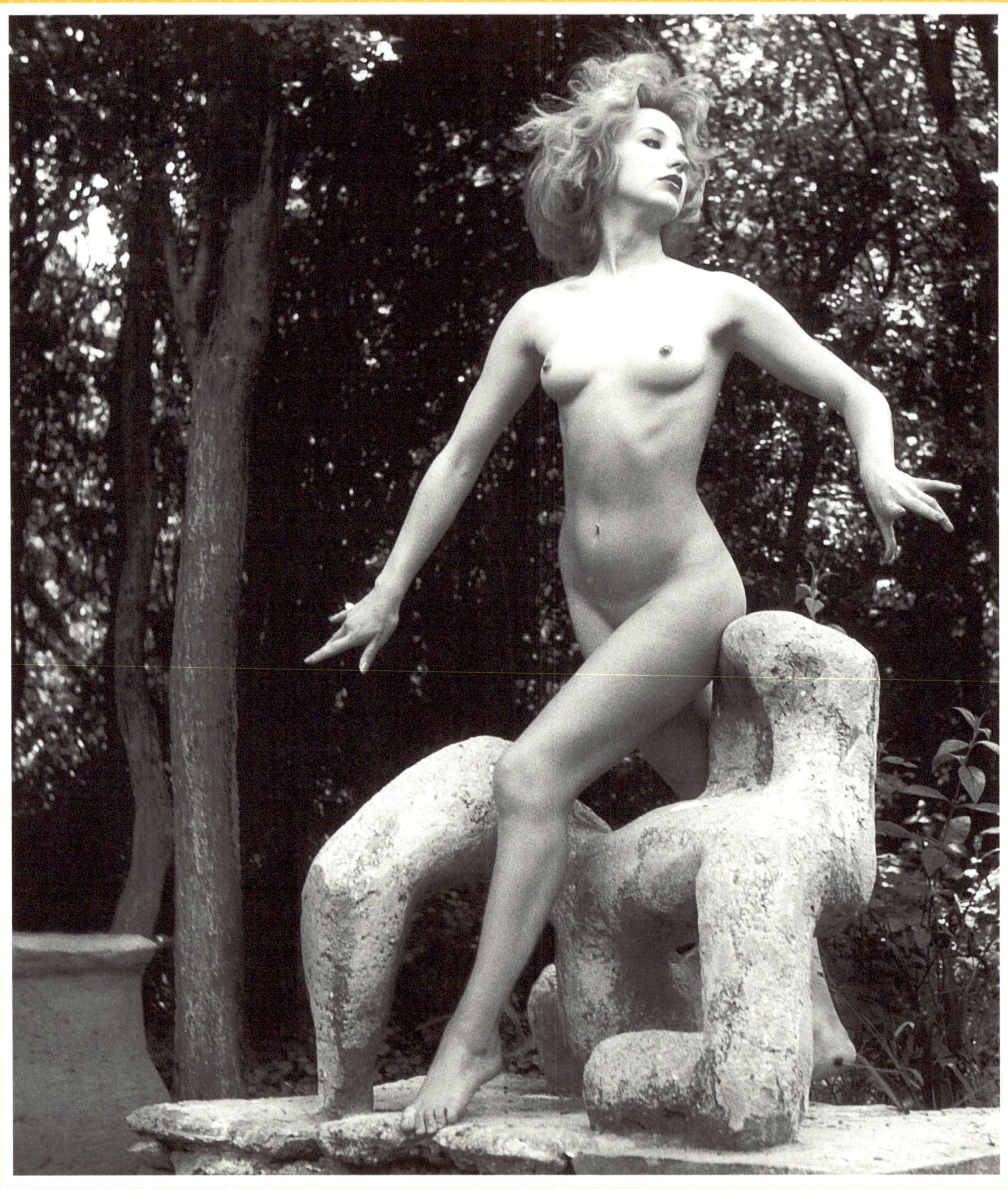

Above and opposite: Bunny Wyatt. Location: Henry Moore Studios and Gardens, Hertfordshire.

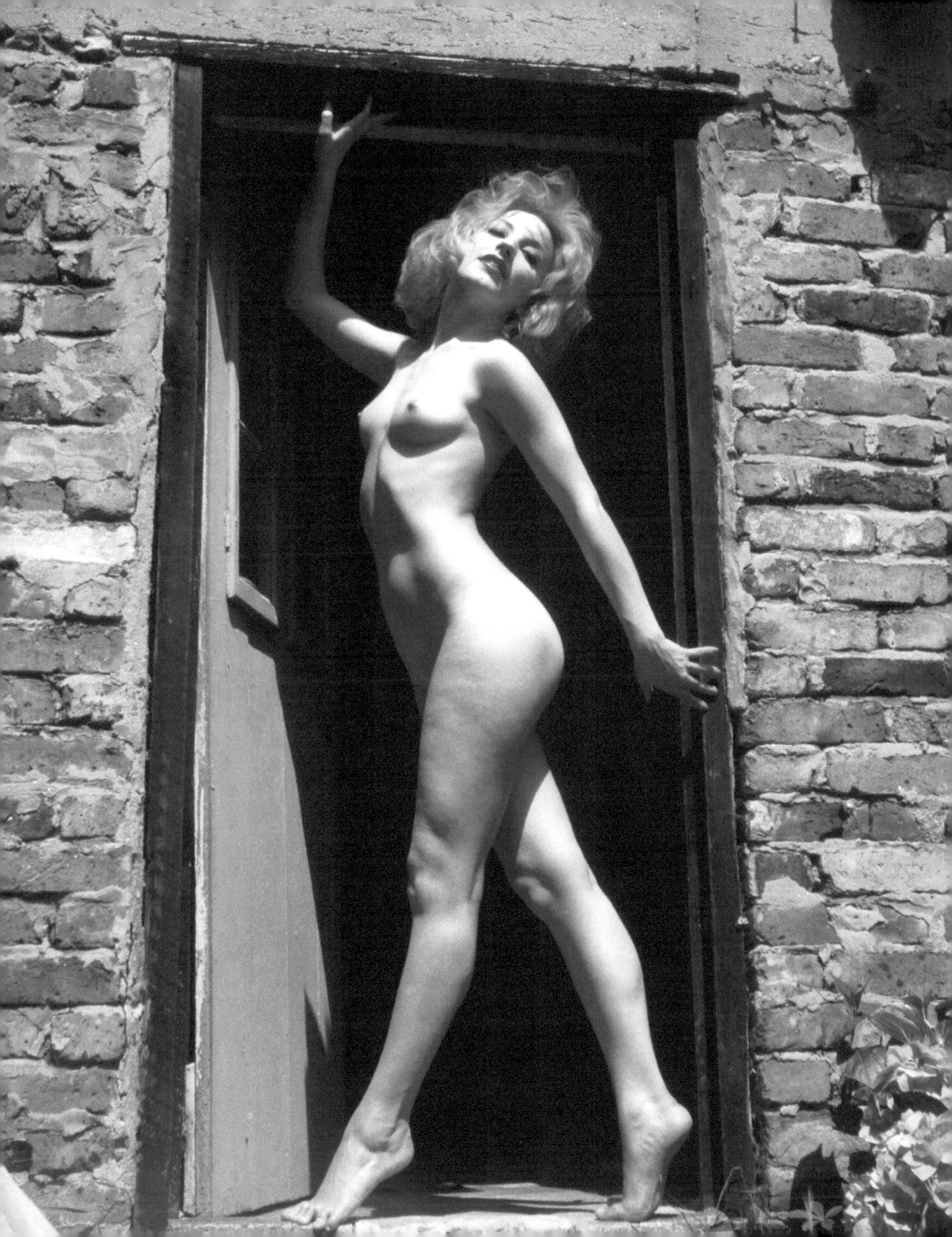

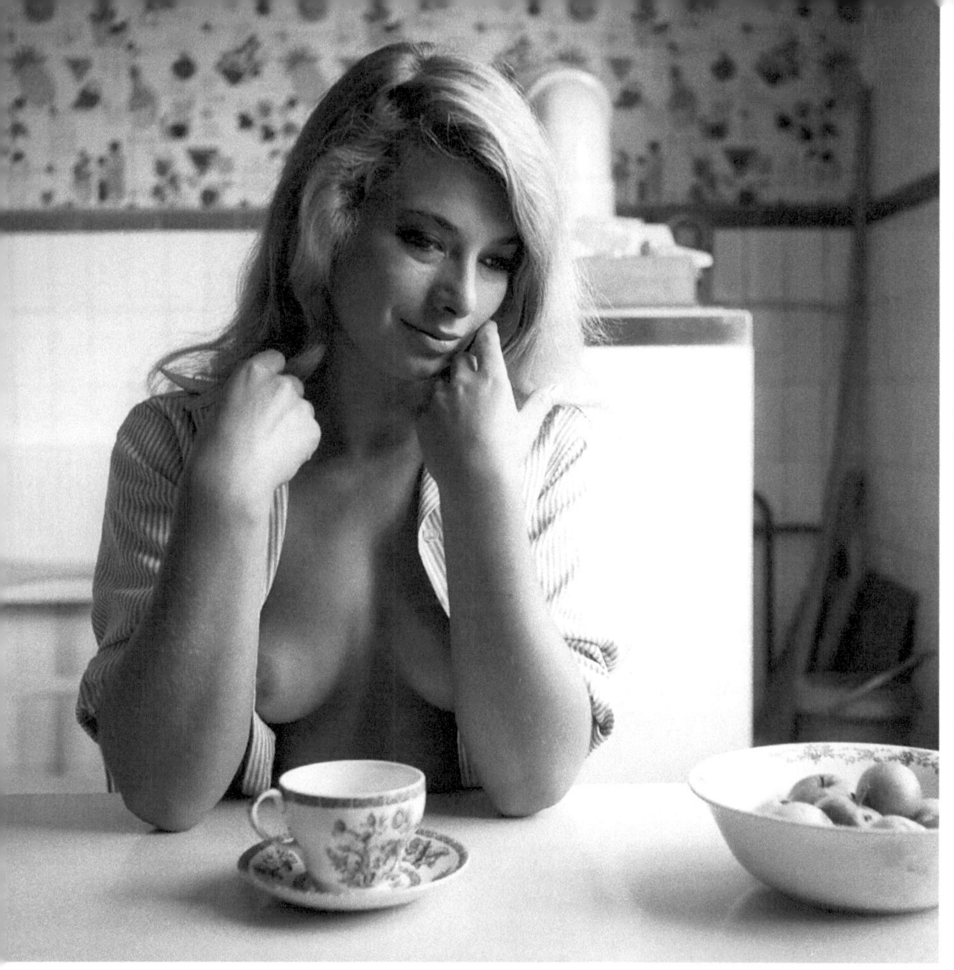

Above and right: Julia.
Opposite: Jackie Aspen.

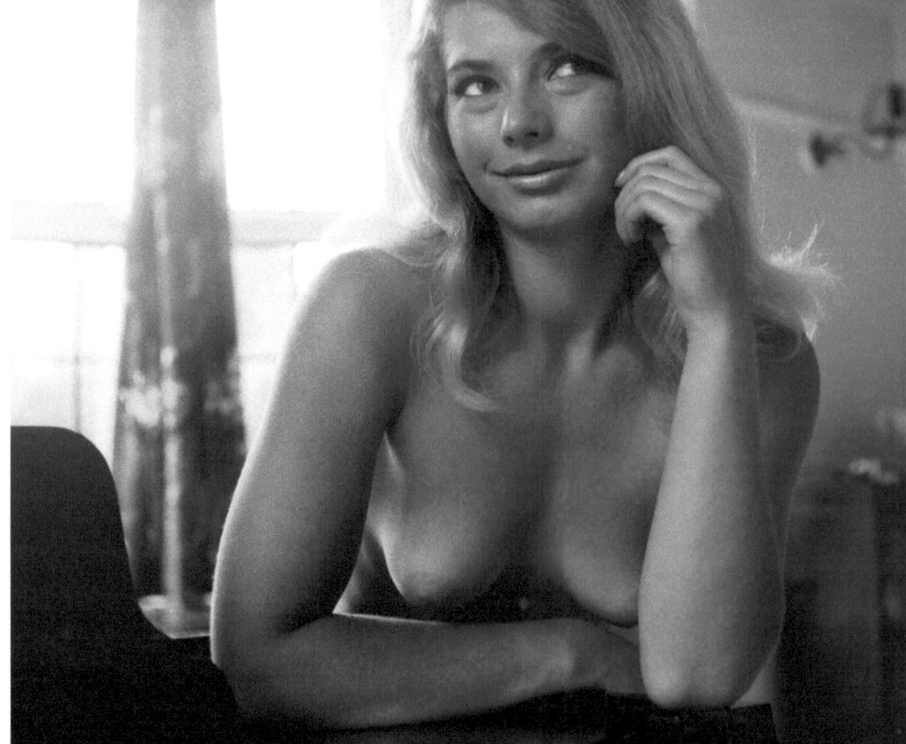

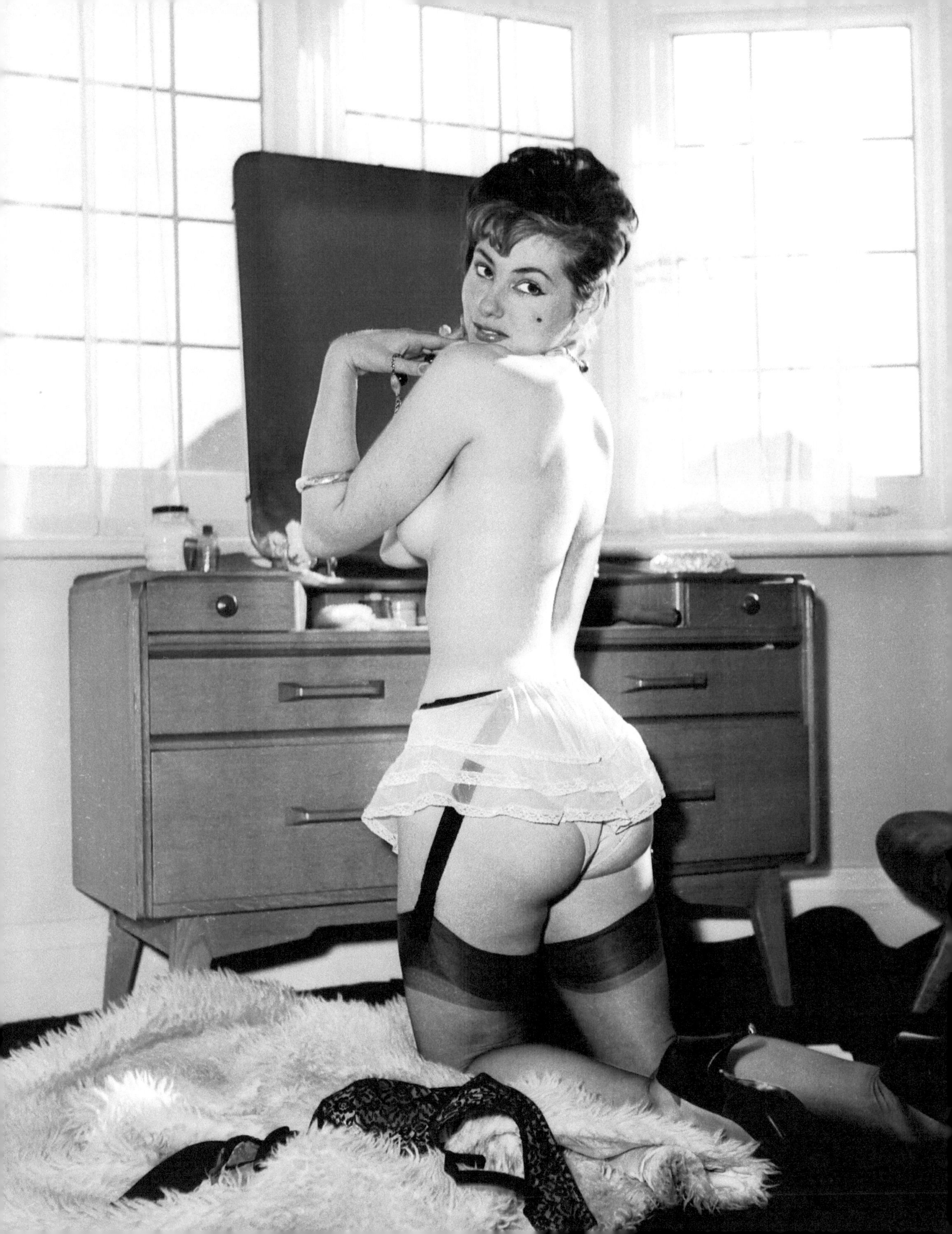

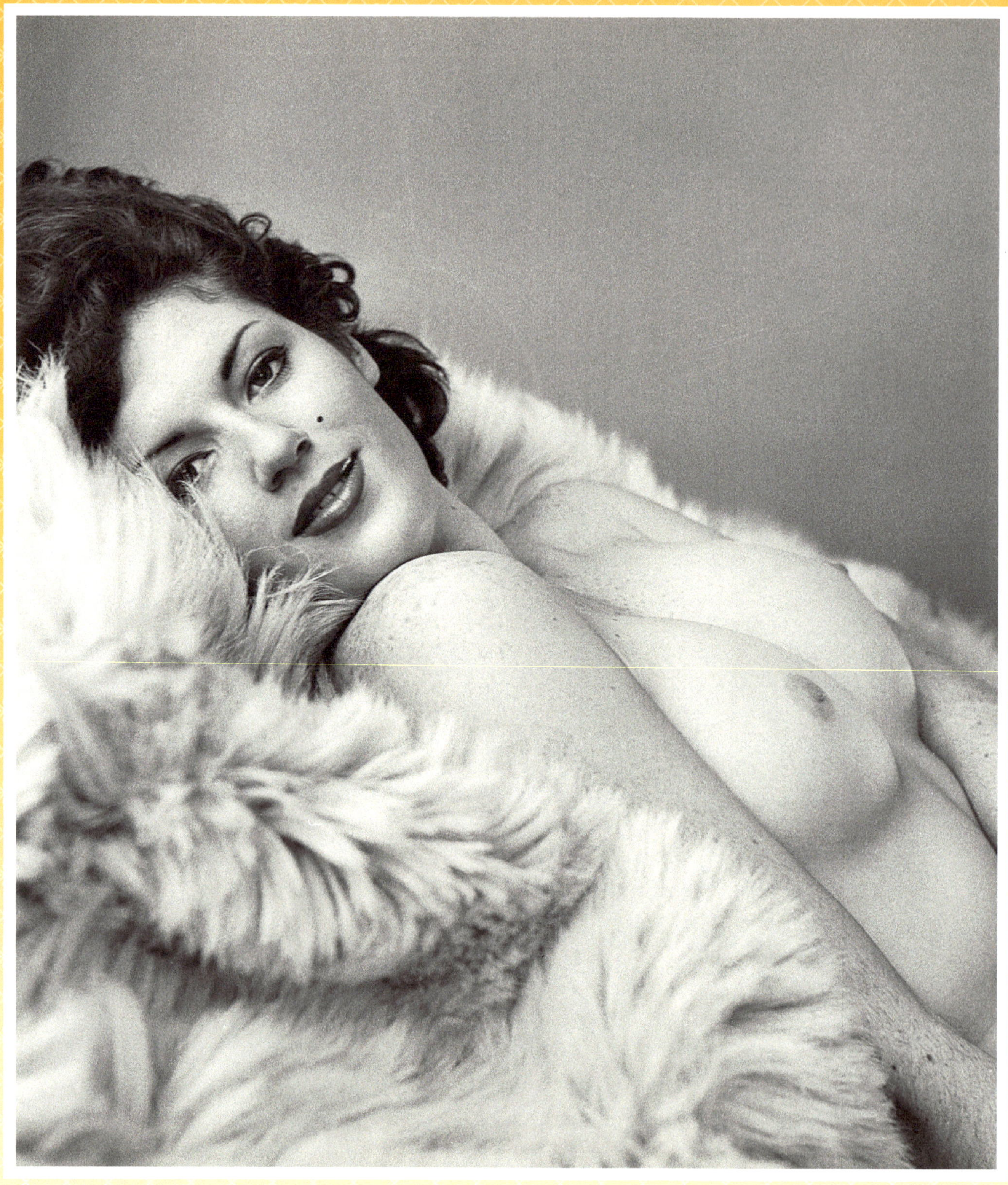

Above and opposite: Maria Clarence.

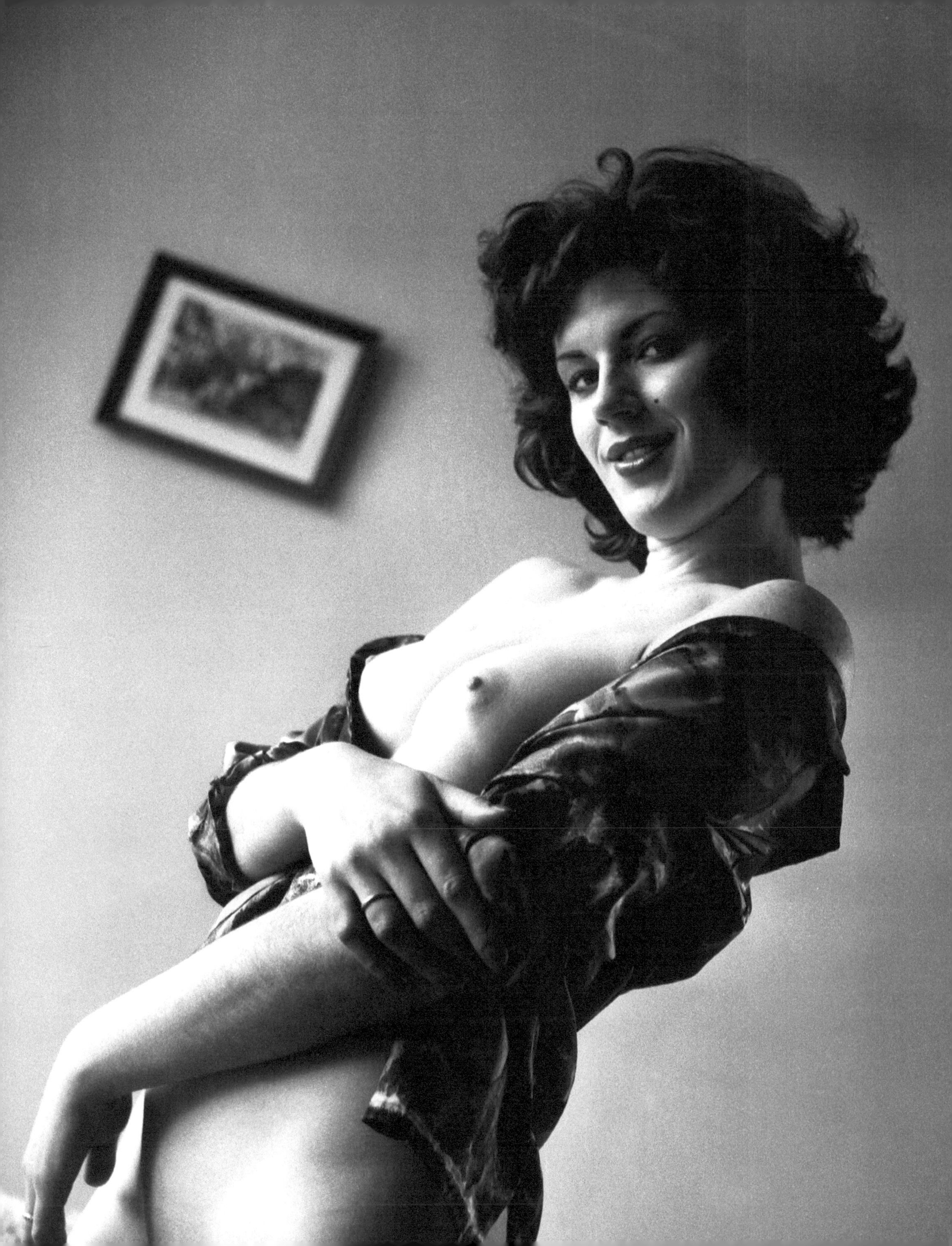

WOLFBAIT
UNDER THE COUNTER CULTURE

ALSO AVAILABLE

Cinema au Naturel

A history of nudist film.

Miniten: Rules of the Game

Invented in the 1930s, Miniten is a
tennis-like game played by naturists.

Naked as Nature Intended

The epic tale of a nudist picture by
Pamela Green, with photographs by
Douglas "Dambuster" Webb, DFM.

The Naked Truth About Harrison Marks

The notorious biography by Franklyn Wood.

Past Masters of the Nude

An illustrated bibliography of nude photography
books published in England from 1896 to 1960.

Slide Show

A luscious look at the photographic slides
of Harrison Marks.

NEW! **X-ray Specs and Other Vintage Ads**

A unique treasure chest of vintage advertising,
full of tease and prurient silliness.

Doing Rude Things

The history of the British sex film.

NEW!

Line and Form

A nostalgic review of Eva Grant's glamour magazine of the 1950s.

NEW!

Glamour Model Revue

Featuring June Palmer, Paula Page and Tina Madison.

THE STEPHEN GLASS COLLECTION

Amazons of Yesteryear

A rare, action-packed collection of images of wrestling women of the 1940s and 1950s.

Beauty Off-Duty

Relaxed, everyday moments caught on camera.

Naked in the Menagerie

A playful look at Eve accompanied by her animal friends.

Nudist Camp Follies – volumes 1 and 2

An intimate look at the natural and free atmosphere in Sun Clubs.

Nymphs and Naiads

Beauty unadorned and outdoors.

Poise and Pose

A magnificent series of photographs of female beauty taken in the studio.

Order online at wolfbait.co.uk

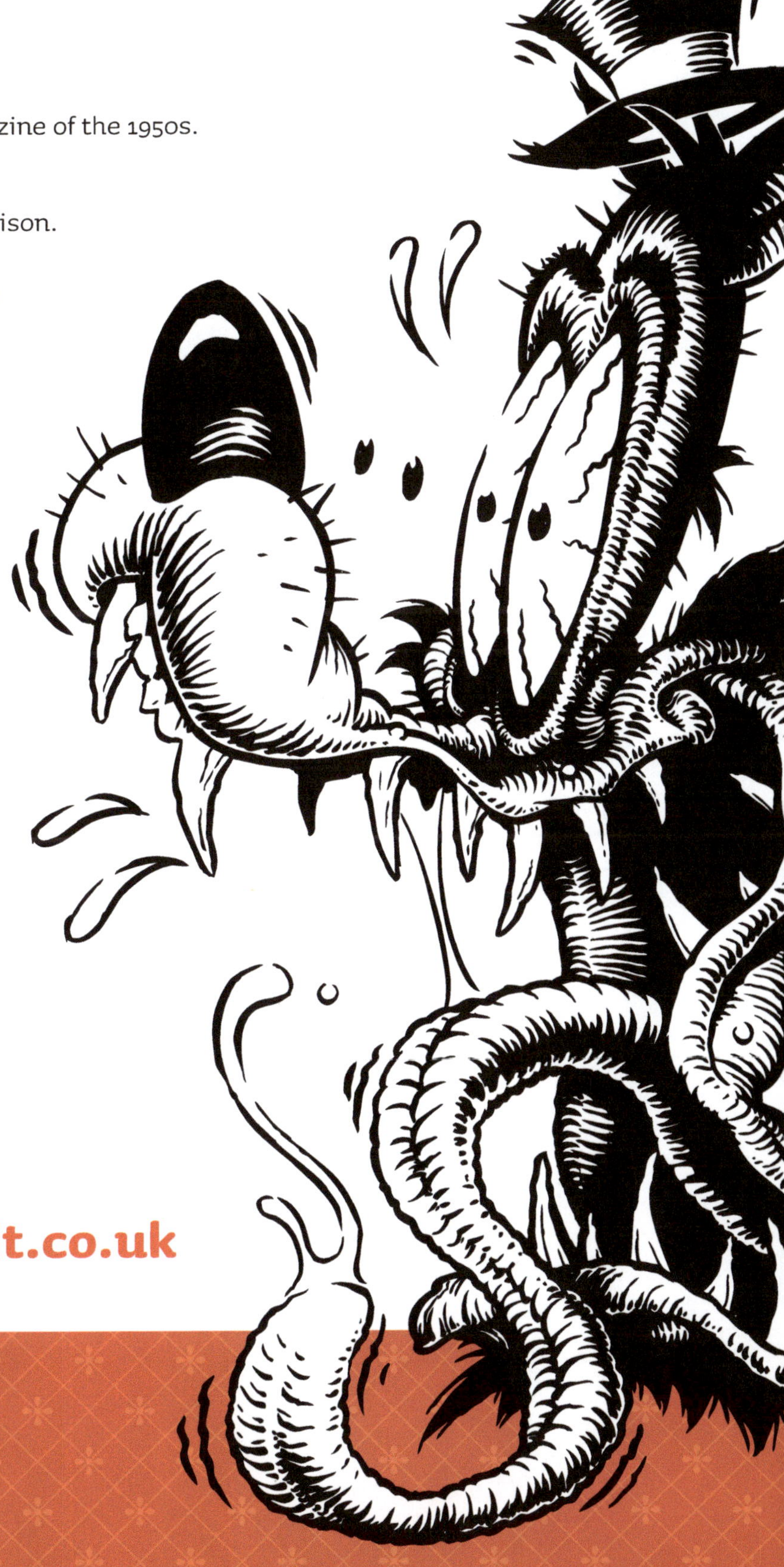

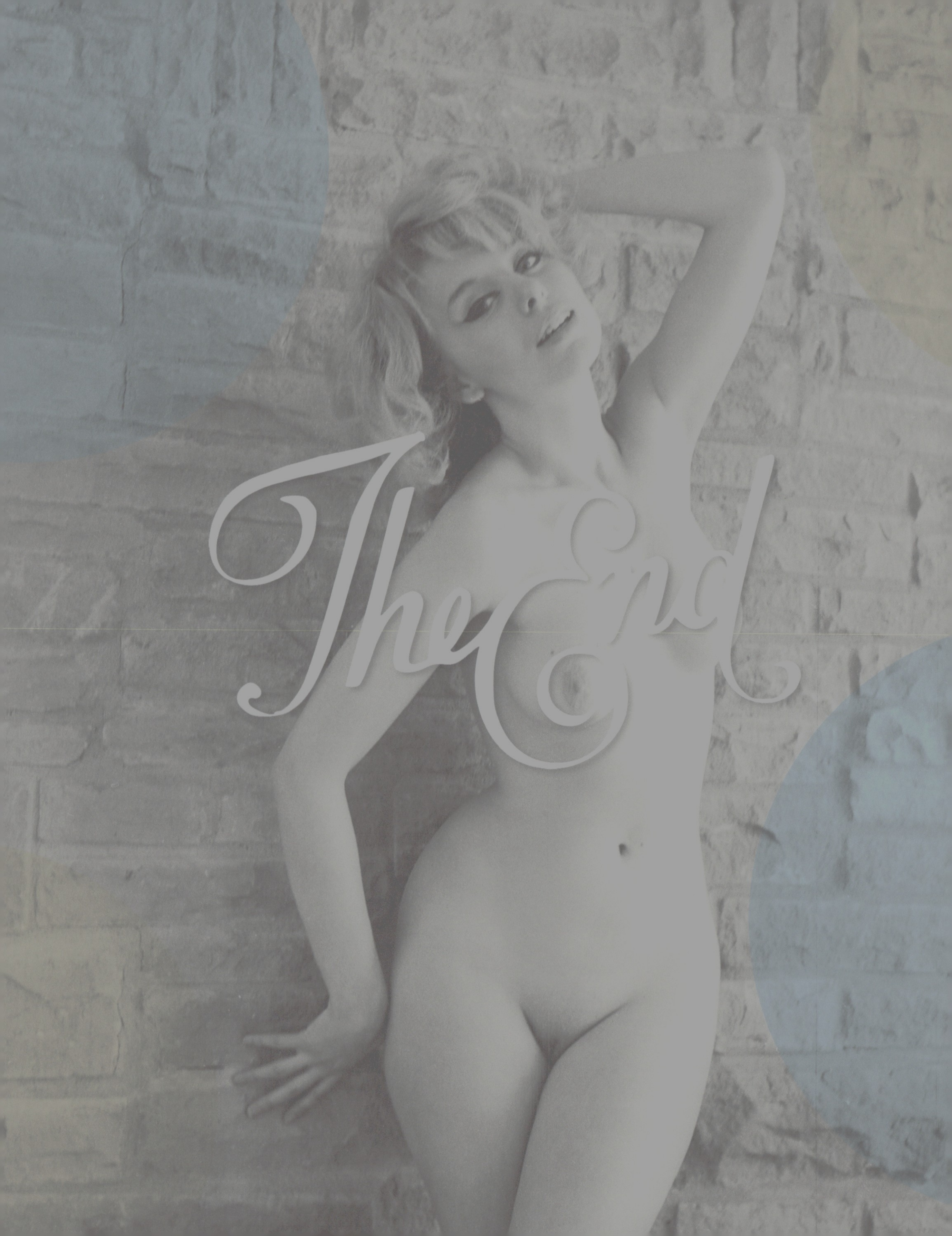
The End

www.ingramcontent.com/pod-product-compliance
Lightning Source LLC
Chambersburg PA
CBHW041946030726
47637CB00010B/29